Lucky Me

"I was getting gas one morning in Branson. A man walked up to me. I could tell he was real excited. He said, "Man, I love your music!" and I humbly said, "Thank you."

The man shook my hand, as he said, "I've got all of your CDs, all of your albums. I've even got some old 8-track tapes of yours. And I want you to know that your show is the greatest!"

I stood there thinking, "Wow, what a way to start my day!"

Then his wife came out and asked him, "Honey, who is that?"

And he yelled back, "Mickey Gilley!"

– Moe Bandy

Lucky Me

Moe Bandy

The Autobiography
With Scot England

Moe Bandy, Lucky Me: The Autobiography

Copyright © 2017 Moe Bandy

Published by:

England Media

102 Rachels Ct Hendersonville TN 37075

(615) 804-0361

englandmedia@yahoo.com

ISBN 978-0-9986367-2-6

Editor: Lindsey McNealy

Cover Design/Layout: Paula Underwood Winters

Printed in the United States of America

For more info on Moe Bandy, including his latest tour schedule, CDs and other merchandise, visit wwww.moebandy.com

DEDICATION

I dedicate this book to my great grandchildren. I know I will have great grandchildren who I will never have the chance to meet. I want my grandchildren's kids to be able to get to know their Grandpa Moe by reading this book.

CONTENTS

FOREWORD

When my husband ran for President in 1988, one of the great mysteries surrounding him was: Does he really like pork rinds, and does he really listen to country music? The national media really didn't believe either. They occasionally accused him of using both to "become a man of the people," as opposed to being the New England blue blood they liked to call him.

What they didn't know was that when we moved to Texas in 1948 and George started his first job in the oil industry, he was basically a traveling salesman. He spent a lot of lonely hours driving the back country roads of West Texas, where the only thing to listen to on the radio was country music.

You could say it was the beginning of a lifelong love affair.

And one of the best things that came out of that affair was our friendship with Moe Bandy.

Like many of the country stars with whom we became friends, the relationship was rather one-sided at first. George loved playing Moe's song "Americana" on the campaign bus during the 1988 presidential campaign. We all knew every word. We had never met Moe, but we sure loved his music.

Thankfully, someone on the campaign called Moe and asked if he would come out on the campaign trail with us. I think he showed up the very next day, and traveled with us off and on that entire fall. My absolute favorite days on the bus were when people like Moe, Loretta Lynn, Crystal Gayle and so many others would travel with us. They made everything more fun, and the jam sessions on the bus were priceless.

Until I read his book, I am not sure I ever knew Moe wanted to be a rodeo cowboy. Thank heavens he decided that was a rather tough way to make a living. All our lives are richer that he picked up a guitar one day and never put it down.

You will love this wonderful story of a Texas boy who never gave up on his dreams. He and his music are true American icons, and we are grateful he came into our lives. When you finish reading his life story, you'll feel like he has come into yours.

Oh, as for the pork rinds – yes, my husband really did love those, too. I now refuse to buy them. But country music will be part of our lives forever.

– Barbara Bush

A MIRACLE IN MERIDIAN

"We don't think we can save the baby, if we are going to save the mother."

♫

I always knew how to make a grand entrance. But on February 12, 1944, my entrance into this world had a little too much excitement.

My mother died as she was giving birth to me. She actually died on the table. But they were able to bring her back. Mother was so young. She was just sixteen, and she was also a very small girl. And I was a very big baby. The doctors told her, "It is either you or the baby. We cannot save both of you."

Mom had had complications leading up to my birth; she had an infection of some kind, and they couldn't do a C-section. The doctor told my dad, "We don't think we can save the baby, if we are going to save the mother." But dad looked at that doctor and said, "I want both of them."

♫

They had to crush my head to get me out. That's when my mom flatlined. The doctors say that it was a total miracle that my mom survived. Later, she told everyone that when she was unconscious, she'd heard the most beautiful music. She said she didn't want to come back. When I started having hit songs, mom said, "Moe, because of you, I have been hearing music since the day you were born."

My mom and dad had gotten married when she was only fifteen. And thirteen months later, she had me. The doctors told her that she should never have another child. But she ended up having five more.

So who would name their kid Moe? Not my mom. My real name is Marion Bandy, Jr., and I was named after my dad. But it was actually my dad who first started calling me Moe. Dad was in the Navy, and there was a guy who he got to be buddies with, and he'd always called my dad

"Moe." So when dad came home from the Navy, he nicknamed me "Moe."

I had a guy come up to me at a concert in Georgia. He said, "I named you Moe." I said, "No you didn't. My dad did." But he said back, "Yes I did. I was in the Navy with your dad." And it turned out that he really was the guy who had started calling my dad "Moe."

My family lived in Meridian, Mississippi until I was six years old. Meridian was a big part of me. It still is. But I was not the first country star to come out of Meridian, Mississippi. Jimmie Rodgers, the man who many call the Father of Country Music, was also from there. Jimmie was nicknamed The Singing Brakeman, because he had worked on the railroad, and he would sing his songs as he worked. My grandfather, Paul Zachary, also worked for the railroad in Meridian at the same time that Jimmie Rodgers did. They worked on different sections of the railroad, and my grandpa never became friends with Jimmie, but he *did* share lots of stories about Jimmie sitting in the boxcars and playing his guitar.

I called my grandpa "Papa." I can still remember him taking me to get a chocolate soda water. I love chocolate soda water! My grandmother's name was Angie, but we called her "Big Mama."

Papa and Big Mama had ten kids, as well as lots of other relatives who would visit or stay with them for extended periods. And those relatives included me. I spent a lot of time with my grandparents. We lived in their big house. Two or three of my aunts also lived there, and we all lived in the same house. We really were one big, happy family.

My grandparents were good people. They were very religious. They had to be in church every Sunday, no matter what. Papa and Big Mama's image was very important to them. They were proud of the reputation they had in town.

But image was not all that important to my father. Dad would come home from the Navy, and go take one of my uncles and just get him drunk as a skunk. They drank moonshine, and Dad would drink enough liquor for the entire town. My dad was as wild as he could be. My mom tried to calm him down, but she couldn't do nothin' with him.

We lived with my grandparents until my dad came back from the war. He had joined the military just after I was born, and he fought in World War Two. When dad came back home, we moved to the little town of Long Creek, Mississippi. It was a suburb of Meridian, and we had a farm there. But my father's side of the family lived in Texas, and dad wanted to go be with them. He wanted to raise cattle.

So when I was six years old, dad and I moved to Texas by ourselves. My mom was pregnant, so she stayed back in Mississippi until my sister was born. Just like after my birth, mom was again told to not have any more children. But she would still end up having four more.

When dad and I first moved to Texas, we lived with my grandmother and my Aunt Melba. We stayed with them until my mother arrived, then we moved to a little place called Macdona, Texas, outside of San Antonio. We lived in a little-bitty shack way out in the country. It was very small. You could almost see through the walls. It was very cold in the winter, and in the summers it became very, very hot.

One of my most vivid childhood memories is from when I started the first grade. We had just moved from Mississippi, so I was the new kid in class... but this was even worse than I thought it would be! Every other kid in class was Mexican. They were all talking in Spanish! I had no clue what was going on. It was like I had landed on Mars. I couldn't understand anyone; it was like I was in a different country. That was a rough time. I ran out of the school building and ran to my aunt's house, but they took me straight back to school and made me stay there. I had a hard time making friends with any of the other kids.

When I was six years old, my parents entered me in a talent contest, where I sang "Goodnight, Irene." And the kids in school finally took to me! They started liking me. That was the first time that I had ever sang in public, but it was just natural to me. My parents started entering me in more talent contests. They would dress me up in little outfits to wear onstage.

Musical talent ran in the family. I was raised in a very musical home. My mom played piano. She played in church when she was younger, but she mainly played at home. Mom sang a lot of gospel songs.

My dad played guitar and played for several bands. He sat in with the Mission City Playboys, and his big claim to fame came when he backed up Gene Autry. They were at the Majestic Theater in San Antonio. That was a big thrill for my dad.

He knew a lot of guitar chords. He was raised with the western swing music around Texas, and he loved all music. But he did have one favorite… Elvis.

Back in the 50s, when I was a kid, one day dad came home and said, "I just heard this guy on the radio and he is incredible! His name is Elvis Presley." My dad loved Elvis. He would sing Elvis songs around the house. Then one day, he found a little band in San Antonio whose lead singer could sing just like Elvis. And my dad was so impressed that he started managing the group. He would get them bookings in different places. Dad loved Elvis, but he never got to see him in concert. I got to see Elvis two times; once in San Antonio, and once in Austin. He had such stage presence! I loved Elvis too.

When my father wasn't playing music, he was a hardworking farmer. Dad and my uncle bought a hay baler, and my dad baled hay for a living. When I was a little kid, just six and seven years old, I would ride on the back of that hay baler. Our farming operation expanded, when my grandpa heard that some people had gotten into a court case. There was a piece of land outside of San Antonio that was tied up in the litigation, and grandpa leased the place while they were fighting over it. There were 1,280 acres on the ranch, and we ended up having it for more than ten years. I rode a horse and worked cattle on that ranch from the time I was eight to sixteen years old.

My Grandpa Bandy was my hero. He was an old cowboy. He could rope cows in the field, and he rode a horse until he was seventy-five years old. He couldn't read or write, but he was one of the smartest men I have ever met. I would read the Bible to him and my grandmother when I was a kid. Grandpa could only scribble his name, "OJ Bandy", but he could trade you out of a horse or cow in a minute.

My grandfather was funny. He would usually drink two Schlitz beers, and no more. He would take me to the local bar, and he would say, "Give me one of them Shits and give this boy one of them Big Reds."

There was a place called "Balls Grocery"; we would go in that store and every single time, my grandpa would say to the owner, "Hello, Mr. Balls. How's your balls?" Grandpa was a very happy guy. He was happy all the time. But my father was not happy all the time... just the opposite.

I remember being in the bars with my dad when I was just a little boy, and whenever I would see him get in an argument with someone, I'd know exactly how it was going to end. The guy he was arguing with would always wind up on the floor, knocked out! Dad had a right hook like a boxer, and I saw him knock so many people out with one punch.

Quite a few men ended up with a broken jaw or a lot of missing teeth thanks to my dad.

Dad was really two people. He was a great man when he was sober, and he did a lot of good for a lot of people. He got jobs for so many men when he went into his sheet metal business. But when he drank, dad became a totally different person. He turned mean. I remember hiding under the table when he was angry. He was really a tough guy. And we all had to be tough to be around my dad.

My dad was quick to dish out very harsh punishment. I got whipped a lot of times by my dad. He was pretty tough on me. I remember a few times when Dad was beating on me, Mom would try to stop him by singing, "There Will Be Peace in the Valley For Me." He worked me over many times. But it made me tough.

We would be out with the horses, and some of them were wild and hadn't been broken yet. Dad would look at me and my brother Mike, and I knew what he was thinking, and I'd secretly hope that he chose Mike. Then he'd yell, "Mike, you ride that horse over there! You ride him or you will have to answer to me."

Dad hit Mike quite a few times. And he hit me even more. With me being the oldest kid, it seemed that dad mellowed a little bit with each new child that was born. But he was pretty rough on the first few boys he had.

My mother was just the total opposite of my dad. She was the nicest, sweetest person you would ever meet in your whole life. She never said one cuss word. The worst thing she ever said was "Shoot." She never tasted even a sip of liquor.

Mom was also a very hard worker. She had six kids in diapers, and she did all the laundry by hand. She would iron clothes all day, she did all the cooking and, was the best cook in the world. And it seemed like she was always doing dishes. She loved to shell peas and snap beans at night as she watched TV.

How my mom got matched up with my dad, I'll never know. My parents were complete opposites, but they loved each other dearly. They were married more than fifty years, until Dad died. Mom never liked my dad's drinking, but she loved him.

We had a balance with our parents. We had a mean father and a sweet mother, so all of us kids ended up being real sweet… as we kicked the crap out of everyone!

Dad was much bigger than me. He stood six feet tall, he was very muscular and had a big build. He didn't believe in taking any lip from anybody, and he wouldn't let his sons take any lip from anybody either. He didn't believe in us kids getting picked on. And if somebody picked on me, I had to take care of it. You had to fight, and you had to win... or you got a bigger fight from Dad when you got home.

One day, I came home with a black eye, and he asked me, "Where'd you get that?" I quietly answered, "A boy hit me."

Dad said, "Did you hit him back?" and I told him, "No. He took off running."

"Well, you hit him back tomorrow," he replied. He just raised us that way.

I had to ride my bike five miles to school each day. I also had a newspaper route. I was a little-bitty guy, and we lived in a rough part of town. One day, along my paper route I rode past another kid who was a hoodlum. He was a bad kid. And he pulled a knife on me and ended up taking all my money.

When I came home, my dad asked, "Where's your money?" I sheepishly said back, "I don't have any. This boy pulled a knife on me and told me to give him all my money."

My dad walked out to his truck and got a big steel pipe. It had lead poured into the end of it. It was about half the size of a baseball bat, and he put the pipe in my bag that I carried all my papers in. Dad said, "This pipe makes you the same size as that boy. And if he has that knife again, this pipe will make you even bigger. You keep this in your bag, and don't ever let someone take your money again."

The next day, I saw the hoodlum coming toward me. I grabbed that pipe and hid it behind my back, and when that kid said, "Give me your money," I hit him with that pipe as hard as I could. He hit the ground and was out like a light. I hopped back on my bike and I took off. From then on, whenever I would pass that kid, he would take off running the other way! That was just the way we were raised.

I was the oldest child in a family of five boys and one girl. My sister, Shirley, was next in line after me. Then my brothers Mike, Rusty, Jimmy and John all came along. And since I was the oldest, if something ever happened to one of my brothers, I had to take care of it. If somebody messed with my sister, I was expected to handle it. And usually that meant beating up the person who was causing the trouble.

One day, a guy slapped my sister at school. And when Daddy found out about it, he came to me and he said, "Moe, you know what to do."

The next day on the school bus, I grabbed that boy and I beat him up. I really beat him. The next day, the boy's mother brought him to school, and she had the shirt he had been wearing the day before; it was covered in blood from the beating I gave him. They called my dad, and when he got to school, he looked at the boy's mom and said, "I'm glad Moe did what he did. And he will do it again if your son ever touches my daughter again."

I ended up being one tough little kid. And the word "little" was especially correct. I was really small. But again, my dad would always give me his words of wisdom like, "There's things that make you just as big as anybody else. You can be the tallest guy in the room, if you have a rock in your hand."

My dad always told me, "You do whatever you need to do to beat the other guy. There is no such thing as a fair fight. Whatever it takes, you do it. And always remember that if someone whips you at school, I'm gonna whip you when you come home."

By the time I'd reached high school, I had survived many street fights. If someone bothered me, I would knock the hell out of 'em. I'm not proud of that, and that's something I never wanted to pass down to my own kids.

I learned how to handle myself at a young age, but I also learned the value of hard work. I always had a job. My paper route was the first, then I worked at a grocery store. In the summer, we'd pick corn. I'd get a little wagon, fill it with corn, and go door to door selling it. I also picked watermelons and sold them on the street.

My dad thought that everyone, no matter how young they were, should work all the time. We didn't have any idle time to do anything. On weekends, we would get up at 6:00 in the morning and work until sundown.

During this time, I was in charge of feeding our cows and hogs, which were a few miles from where we lived. When I was fourteen, I was driving our old pickup truck to go and do the feeding. But once when I was at a stop sign, I started talking to a friend of mine. Right then, my foot slipped off the brake and I ended up hitting another car. My friend ran away. But I stayed there and waited for the police. When they came, they asked me, "How old are you, and do you have a license?" to which I said, "No I don't. I'm fourteen." They called my dad and told him I shouldn't be driving. I got a real good whipping for that one.

But my mother did save me from one whipping. My brother Rusty was snooping in my bedroom drawer one day and he found a pack of cigarettes. He was headed to tell on me when I grabbed him. I made him eat one of the cigarettes. I told him I would feed them to him until he promised not to tell on me. After the first one, he gave me his word. But, as soon as I let him up, he headed straight to mom and told on me. And he also told her about me making him eat a cigarette. But he sure was shocked when mom responded, "Well, Rusty, you shouldn't have been goin' through Moe's drawer."

My parents had six kids, but they actually raised seven. There was a boy my age named Donald French. We called him Frenchy. He came to our house one day, selling soap out of a wagon. We were going out to the ranch to work our cattle, and he asked if he could go with us. And from that day on, he stayed with us. My parents (who already had six kids) raised him too! He was like my brother. Frenchy was a real scrawny guy, even more than me!

Frenchy and I were both fifteen years old when my parents decided to visit some relatives back in Mississippi. Dad thought we were old enough to leave by ourselves, so, as he and mom left, he gave us fifty dollars and sternly told us, "Don't be getting into any trouble."

As mom and dad were pulling out of the driveway, Frenchy asked me, "Hey, would you like to go to Mexico? We can drink alcohol there. And I've heard they have these hookers…" I looked at the fifty dollars Dad had just put into my hand. But for some reason I couldn't remember the words he told me as he gave me the money!

Me and Frenchy jumped in our old '55 Chevrolet pickup (my family used the truck to haul hogs) and we drove that truck all the way to Mexico. And we had a big time! As soon as we got there, we walked into a bar and I said to the bartender, "We want two whiskey sours." Why I ordered that, I will never know. I guess I had heard it in the movies. But we got so drunk. Frenchy passed completely out.

We did manage to get back home before my parents did, but the first thing my dad asked me was, "Where is the fifty dollars?" I have no idea why I told him the truth. But I did.

"We used it when we went to Mexico," I quietly said. My Dad gave us hell over that.

But surprisingly, my parents left me and Frenchy alone once again the next summer. My family was in the process of building a Jim Walters home. You bought the house frame, and then you finished the interior on your own. Our house was not quite finished when my parents left on vacation.

So, as soon as mom and dad drove away, Frenchy and I started planning to throw a party. A good friend of mine, Jimmy Deason, came over and the party was on. All of our friends came over and we had a big time. Jimmy found a ladder that was standing in a room that Dad was still working on, and while the rest of us were busy partying, he climbed up the ladder and went into the attic. He ended up staying up there so long that he fell asleep. A short time later, there was a huge crash in the living room. Jimmy had fallen down out of the attic, right down into the middle of the living room! And when he fell, he brought down all the sheet rock, plaster and everything from the ceiling. I said, "My dad is going to absolutely kill me!" After we sent everyone home, me and Frenchy ended up getting some sheet rock and redoing all of that damage. We got it finished before my parents came home, and my dad never noticed anything.

Frenchy and I had some great times as we were growing up. But Frenchy had a heart attack and passed away a few years ago.

When I was in junior high school, I played football, and I found out that I was very good at it. My toughness helped, and the work ethic my dad had taught me was also a big benefit. I was the quarterback, and was also named captain of the team. I've still got my Hot Wells Blue Devils jacket with the little star that means I was the captain.

When I got to high school, a coach from Burbank High saw me, and asked if I would come play for them. Burbank was a school across town, and I ended up playing there. But even though I was pretty hot stuff, I had one major problem… I never grew! I stayed small. But I loved taking part in sports of all kinds.

With all of my previous fighting experience, I figured that I would make a good boxer, too, so I joined the boy's club and boxed a little bit. But I was so small, and we had to wear these huge gloves; I could hardly hold my arms up! And I quickly found out that I couldn't kick 'em or bite 'em, or bend their fingers back until they broke, like I was used to doing whenever I'd be in a street fight. So I continued looking for a sport that I would be a good fit for.

That sport turned out to be rodeo. When I was six years old, my grandfather had me riding little calves that we had on our farm. And now that I was older, Frenchy and I had decided to try to ride bulls. To practice, we built us a bucking barrel. It was a big barrel, like a trash or oil barrel, that we tied to a tree. It really looked like a bull, and was a great way to learn.

We started going to youth rodeos, and I entered the bull riding and bareback bronc riding competition. Frenchy had an old Ford Falcon. It looked good, but we ended up pushing that thing further than we drove it. It always broke down on us. It was especially bad after we had been at a rodeo, and we'd get all banged up, getting thrown off the bulls. We were sore all over, and then we'd end up having to push Frenchy's car home.

I continued riding bulls as I got ready for the next football season. But then my coach called me and told me I could not play anymore. He said that, since I had won a little money (very little) in the rodeo, I was now considered a professional athlete.

During my senior year at East Central High School, I met the girl who would become my wife. Margaret was in my class, when I happened to get a part in the senior play. I really liked her, and I knew that she was in the crowd on performance night. After the play was over, I ran around the building to catch her, and when I did, I asked her to the prom. I was thrilled when she said yes.

In 1962, as soon as I had gotten my diploma, I moved to Temple, Texas to work for my dad. By then, he had gotten a job as a sheet metal worker. He was with a big construction company now, and we helped build the Scott and White Hospital in Temple. My best friend Johnny Blocker moved to Temple with me, where he and I shared a little apartment with another young guy, Albert Mahalski. We all lived there together for a year.

But while I was doing construction all week, each weekend I would drive back home so I could date Margaret. A year after our graduation, on May 4, 1963, we got married. We were both nineteen years old. We would be together for the next thirty-three years.

Margaret and I had been married for a little more than a year when our first child was born. My daughter Laura was the first of three children for Margaret and me. Our second child, Ronnie, was born in 1966. But it would be another ten years before we were blessed with our third child, Lisa, who was born in April of 1976.

FROM SHEET METAL TO STARDOM

I served a four-year apprenticeship as a sheet metal worker, where I made duct work for air conditioning and heating. Then I helped install it in buildings. We worked on lots of commercial buildings, and I worked my way up and became foreman for some big building projects in San Antonio.

For the first couple years of my construction career, I also still kept my dream alive of becoming a rodeo star. I never took any real bull riding lessons, unless you count the barrel tied to the tree. I just started riding. But I was not as good as I wanted to be, and bull riding is a sport that you had better be good at. If not, you will end up getting hurt. I once had a bull throw me, and it broke my collarbone. Then he stuck a horn in several of my ribs. The doctor put a figure-eight wrap on me for my broken collarbone, and the next week I entered the bull riding again. And, once again, I got thrown and it broke my collarbone again.

So that was my last ride. I was twenty years old. I said, "I need to do something else." That "something else" turned out to be music. I went and bought me a guitar, and I started playing it. My friend Johnny Blocker also had a guitar, and we practiced together. I spent every night trying to get better at my singing and guitar playing. And then… I had a truly life-changing experience. Hank Thompson came to town.

Hank Thompson was booked to play at a local club, and me and some of my buddies from work went to see him. I was sitting front and center when he walked onstage. He had one of his fanciest and best outfits on. And when he started singing, I was in awe! Hank had his huge band, the Brazos Valley Boys. And his show was unbelievable.

Later, during the show, the guys I was with said, "We need to go." I told them, "Not me! I'm staying right here. I'll get a ride home." I sat there and watched Hank, and it was a changing point in my life. It was like a religious experience. I knew that this was what I wanted to do, and I said to myself, "Whatever it takes, I've got to do that."

From that point on, I dreamed of walking onstage just like Hank did. I dreamed of smiling and waving at the crowd like he did. Hank Thompson was the first star that I ever saw in concert, and many years later, I was finally able to tell that story to Hank. Every time I worked with him, I would tell him that story. I am still great friends with Hank's widow, Ann.

Once I had started playing music, I knew that it was something I wanted to do in a big way. It was just an unbelievable feeling to get paid (no matter how small the amount) to play music!

I went down to a bar called The Pleasant Hill Tavern, where it had a little outdoor patio, and I told the owner that my buddies and I had been playing music at our house. The owner said, "Bring your guitars up here and sit on the patio." So we went up there and started playing, and the people loved us! It was the first time I had ever heard applause in my life.

I had been insecure and shy about playing in front of anyone, but when I heard that applause, I thought, "Wow. These people really like me." The manager said, "Y'all come back tomorrow night and I'll give you $5.00 apiece and all the beer you can drink." We jumped at the offer!

But the free beer ended at the end of the next night. We drank him under the table! But me and my buddies, Bill Stein, Bobby Graham and Mack Arnold started playing there on a regular basis, and people started coming out just to hear us. And even though we had a terrible band, the people loved it.

I soon put together a little band called Moe Bandy and the Country Partners. We had matching shirts and little ties. The band was horrible. But those fellas were really good guys. I still keep up with some of them.

I lived in a district that had a big Polish population, and we were hired to play at a lot of weddings. Even though I'm not Polish, I got hired to play at a lot of Polish weddings. We were playing at weddings almost every Saturday night in May, June and July. We didn't play Polish music, we were doing all country music. We played Merle Haggard. Merle had just come out. We played George Jones. George was my all-time hero, and I knew all of his songs. I even had a flat-top haircut and sideburns like he had at the time. We also played Ernest Tubb. Those were all the stars that I loved, and all people who I had no idea that I would get to work with in the years to come.

Lucky Me by Moe Bandy

We loved playing for weddings, but later in my career, I actually played for a divorce! A man was a big fan of mine, and he wanted to have a big party to celebrate his divorce. He went through my booking agency, and paid my usual fee for us to play at his divorce party. As I sang my songs, he danced with every woman who was there. It was the best divorce celebration I have ever been a part of.

I enjoyed playing with The Country Partners. But then, I saw an advertisement for a group called The Mavericks, saying that they needed a singer. So I called them up and went for a try out. And they just went nuts over me! So I joined The Mavericks. And eventually, we renamed the group "Moe Bandy and The Mavericks."

We had some great times back in the 60s. My little band was not the hottest band around, but we played a lot of local gigs. There were other local bands that were more popular than us, and those bands would hardly talk to us. We would do a benefit where all the bands played together, and some of the other bands would kind of look down at us. But a few years later, when I got my first hit records, those bands tried to act like they were my best friends.

One of my true best friends was Forest Culpepper. Forest played steel guitar for me when I first started out, and we told each other that we were going to play together for my entire career. But he fell in love and got married, worked his way through college and became an architect.

I wasn't playing any shows more than fifty miles from where I lived, but I got the idea that I needed a bus. I thought that, if Hank Thompson had a bus, then I should too! So, I bought an old Army bus. My pal Forest Culpepper was also an engineer, and he told me that he could convert the bus for us. The first thing he did was paint the entire bus purple! And it looked terrible! He also put plaster up through the entire inside of it. It looked like a cave, and that plaster ended up falling off all over us. We also blew the engine in the bus. Yes, I was officially a country music singer!

We once played a place called Shady Acres, just outside of San Antonio. They called one day and asked if we could back up some big name artists. Our band was so bad, we were really bad. But I told them, "Of course we can back up other folks!" The first star that we backed up was Stonewall Jackson. He was also the first star I ever met. What a thrill that was.

We also played for Loretta Lynn. She walked in, and her husband Mooney was carrying her guitar. They were on tour, just traveling the country, using any local band that she could find. About ten years later, we did another show together. By then, I was a star, and Loretta was an even bigger star. And I was totally shocked, when Loretta said, "My mother would love to meet you, Moe! You are her favorite singer."

In the early days, we backed up Charley Pride, played for Mel Street, and we backed up Rusty and Doug Kershaw a couple times. They were all coming in, and none of them had a band at that time.

Wynn Stewart was one of my all-time heroes. He probably impressed me more than any other entertainer. And I got to work with Wynn and get to know him. We backed him up twice. And he was the singer's singer. All the singers loved him. The last time I got to see him was when I played a club in Amarillo. I was pretty hot at the time; I had a big crowd. And Wynn came out to see me. We sat on my bus and drank whiskey all night long, as we played guitar and sang. We had a ball.

By then, my little band was coming along. We weren't great, but we were better than when we first started! I ran into a man in San Antonio who told me, "I want to make a record on you." I ended up paying for the recording session, as well as for five hundred records. I wrote almost every song on that album we did. One of those songs was called "Lonely Girl", and one day, I was driving in my car when "Lonely Girl" came on the radio. I pulled over to the side of the road. I was so excited, I started trembling. I couldn't believe it! When I got home, everyone was calling me, saying, "Do you know your song was on the radio?!"

KBER in San Antonio played "Lonely Girl." And KBUK played it. Then, I started my first "radio promotion tour." I filled my car up with the five hundred records I had pressed up, and I drove all over Texas. I would stop at each radio station and ask them to play my record. You could tell from their reactions that most of them were probably not going to play it. I went to WBAP, which was the big station in Texas at the time. Bill Mack was the main guy there. They wouldn't even let me in. But later on, I got to be dear friends with Bill Mack. After I had made it big, I always ribbed Bill by saying, "Yeah, you wouldn't let me in back then. Remember that?" Bill and I have become very good friends over the years.

I had better luck when I visited a station in Robstown, Texas. I walked in, and confidently announced: "My name is Moe Bandy and this is my new record," (I didn't tell them it was my ONLY record!) The guy who was on the air smiled big and said, "I sure will play it! Let's put it on right now." And by golly, he put it on and played it right then! That DJ's name was Cecil Martin. Years later, I was in Fort Worth doing a show and another act walked in. It was a guy dressed like a hobo, wearing baggy overalls, and with a scruffy beard. The man walked up to me and asked, "Do you remember me?" I said, "No, I'm sorry I don't."

He said, "I played your record when you brought it in. My name is Cecil Martin... but now you can call me Boxcar Willie."

Of course, many years later, Boxcar Willie would become one of the first acts to make it big in Branson, Missouri. He was there before me. But once I moved to Branson, Box and I became very close friends as well.

I'd also like to say another thing about Boxcar: Boxcar never had a hit song in the U.S., but in Europe, he was like Elvis. I did a show in Frankfort Germany with him, where we played a big hall that Hitler had given speeches in. The Bellamy Brothers were also on the show. The Bellamys were very popular over there, and they tore the crowd up. And then Boxcar Willie came out, and it was like Elvis had walked out on stage! That place went berserk. It was unbelievable.

One day, a man called and said, "We need you and your band to back up some guys in Fort Worth, and then in Lubbock, Texas."

We thought, "Wow! We are going on the road!" We went to Fort Worth and backed up Webb Pierce at Panther Hall, and we were so nervous. We probably would have played better if we had downed a few drinks to calm our nerves. But it was the star of the show who did most of the drinking that night. After the show, when Webb was signing autographs, he handed his guitar to someone. And they ran off with it. Then Webb accused me of stealing it! He told me, "Just give me the strap back and you can keep the guitar." But I finally convinced him that I didn't take it.

The next day, we drove to Lubbock and did a show with Bob Wills, Tex Ritter and Jim Ed Brown. It was unbelievable! We did two shows that day, and in between shows I listened as Tex Ritter and Bob Wills talked about some movies that they had been in. I ate it up, and I kept thinking, "I am backing up Bob Wills!" What a thrill.

At each show, I would do one song, and then I would introduce the rest of the show, and my band would play back up for everyone. Bob didn't have his band back then; it was just him and Tag Lambert. Many years later, when I became friends with Jim Ed Brown, I talked to him about those shows, and he actually remembered them. I was so in awe of all of those people.

David Barton played bass for Jim Ed Brown during that show in Lubbock, and after the show, David told me that he would like to do a recording session with me in Nashville. There was one catch, though: I had to pay for all of the recording expenses. I jumped at the chance! I had never been to Tennessee, and I couldn't wait to get there!

But I wasn't going to drive to Nashville like all the other country music dreamers. I was going to go in style. I was going to fly! I purchased my very first airplane ticket. I was scared to death to fly, and as we were sitting in the plane, fixin' to take off, they announced over the intercom: "Good morning. This is a breakfast flight." I was so nervous that when the stewardess came by and asked me, "What is your destination?" I said, "Two eggs over easy, with ham!"

In 1967, I heard that a local TV show was searching for a band to back up all the country artists who were going to appear on a weekly program called Country Corner. I contacted the show's producers, and Moe Bandy and the Mavericks landed the gig! We were gonna be TV stars!

A furniture store was the sponsor of the show, and the store owner would come out and sell furniture in between songs. It was a pretty rough show, but one bright spot was a girl singer who was a regular on the program. She went by one name: Dottsy. She was eleven or twelve years old, and she ended up having some national hit songs.

I got to do a couple songs every week on the show. I don't know if that helped or hurt my career! I had never done television before, but it was good practice. And since the show was on at the same time as Johnny Carson's Tonight Show, not a lot of people were watching.

Moe Bandy and the Mavericks also had a running engagement at the Skyline Club in Austin, Texas. You could find us playing there every Wednesday night. But I always wondered how smart that was. The Skyline Club was the last place that Hank Williams played just before his death. And then, seven years later, it would be the last place that Johnny Horton performed, just before he was killed in a car accident. Luckily, I survived the Skyline Club curse! Unfortunately though, the club didn't survive. They eventually tore it all down and built a CVS store in its place.

Being a country singer at the honky-tonks and bars in Texas could be a little dangerous. When I was first starting out, lots of fights would break out while we were singing (I hope it wasn't my singing that started the fights!).

One night, I was playing a club outside of San Antonio, when a fight started. And it was just like in the movies, with everybody fighting. Everyone was hitting someone. I was up on stage trying to stay out of it. The crowd fought and fought and fought. And I had the mic stand in my hand, in case someone jumped up on stage. There was blood all over the place. But when they got it cleaned up, we started playing again just like nothing had ever happened.

In 1972, I met the man who would play a very important role in my life; his name was Ray Baker. I was working at my sheet metal job, when a co-worker told me that a record producer was coming to town. Ray Baker was that producer, and he was coming to San Antonio on a hunting trip. My friend knew where Ray was staying, and as soon as he told me, I headed straight there.

I knocked on Ray's door, and when he opened it I said, "My name is Moe Bandy. I'm playing in town tonight, and would like you to come hear me." And he did! At the end of the night, Ray offered to do a recording session on me... if I agreed to pay for it all. Once again, I was the one who had to come up with the money for my recording sessions, but I happily agreed to it!

On April 4, 1972, I had a recording session at Music City Recorders in Nashville. The company was owned by the legendary Scotty Moore, who played guitar for Elvis in the 1950s. Since this was my first real session, I was a nervous wreck. When Scotty said that he would play guitar on my session, I got even more scared. My producer finally walked into the studio and asked me, "Do you drink?"

I said, "Yeah."

He said, "Let's go have a couple drinks of whiskey."

I was so in awe of being in a real studio in Nashville. We recorded a couple songs, and they got played around Texas a little bit, but I was still not able to quit my day job. I played music almost every night, but I was still working at my sheet metal job during the day. I had to keep that job, especially since I had a growing family. Margret and I had a baby girl, and then a baby boy.

We ended up doing several more recording sessions in Nashville, and each time I would leave for Music City, my wife would remind me of all of our daily bills. I was making a pretty good living in construction, but coming up with the money to pay for all my recording sessions was getting harder and harder. My wife and I argued many times over me spending our money on my country music dream.

When the time came for me to pay for my latest recording session with Ray, I had spent almost all of the money that I had. Over the years, there have been some stories that said that I had actually sold my furniture to pay for the session. That is not exactly true; I didn't sell the furniture, but I *did* borrow against it. I took out a loan and put my furniture up as collateral.

So, I went for broke. I put everything I had on one last recording session. And it went very well. One of the songs we recorded was called "I Just Started Hatin' Cheatin' Songs Today." Everyone in the studio thought it was a good song.

But when we were finished with the session, I thought that my music career was, too. I was frustrated, and I was at the end of my rope. I was twenty-nine years old and I was totally out of money. My Dad had a solution, as he yelled at me, "You need to take that damn guitar and wrap it around a tree! You need to think of your family. You need to pay attention to your trade. You are a sheet metal worker!"

I knew Dad was right. One day, I went to him and I said, "I'm quitting the music business. I've tried it and it ain't workin'." Dad slapped me on the back and said, "Good! That's real good. I'm gonna get you runnin' the big jobs." And he did. I ended up having 15 to 20 men working for me as we built high rise buildings.

And right when I had given up on the music business… Ray Baker called me. Ray said, "Moe, remember that song we recorded, 'I Just Started Hatin' Cheatin' Songs Today'? That song is starting to get some action out there on the radio!" It had started taking off, and Ray started trying to pitch me to a major record label. He went to RCA. There was a guy named Wally Cochran there, and Wally said, "I want to sign Moe to RCA." But before we could complete the deal, Wally left the record label.

He ended up going to Atlanta, where he helped start a label called GRC. GRC stood for General Recording Corporation. The man who owned GRC was an underworld character. We didn't know it at the

My Grandpa.
My hero.

Dad and Grandpa
take care of our
cattle

My dad and granddad
in the late 50s.
These were real
cowboys.

Mom and Dad

Moe Bandy's first photo shoot, 1944

6 months old

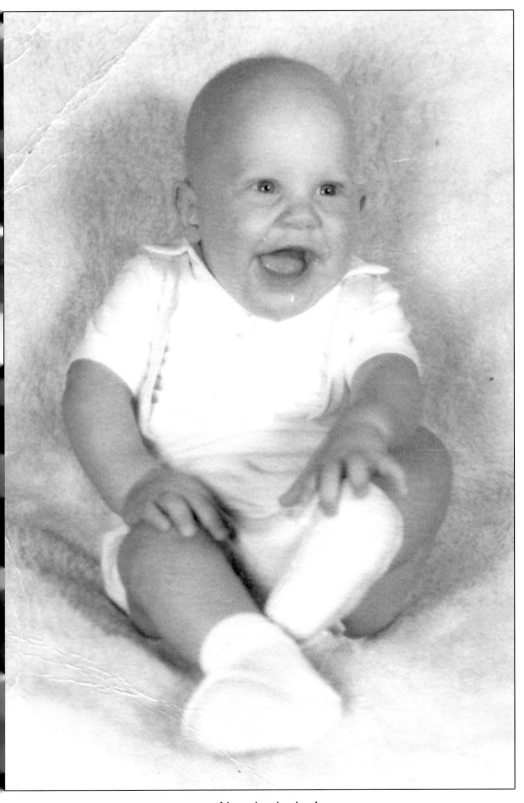

Already singing!

With Mom and Dad

Playing cowboy with my grandpa Bandy.

Dad and me

Wearing my first
cowboy hat!

Before I rode bulls, I apparently rode giant rabbits! My rodeo pals will kill me when they see the sandels I wore!

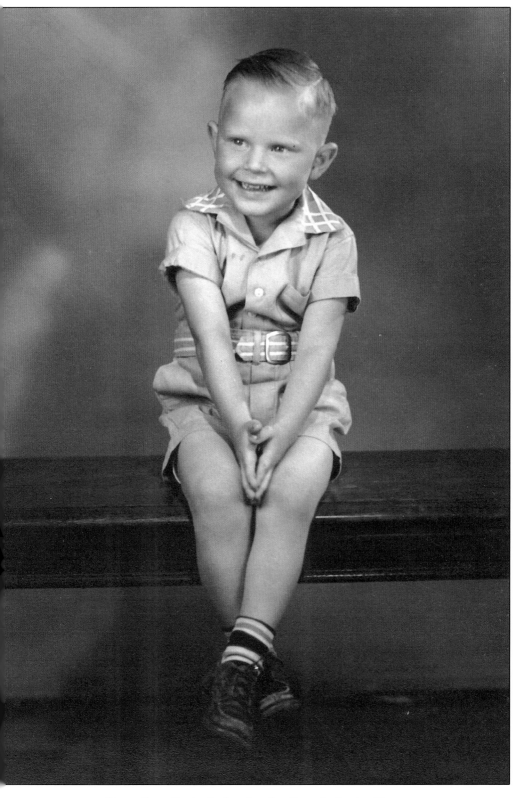

One of my first photo shoots. San Antonio, Texas

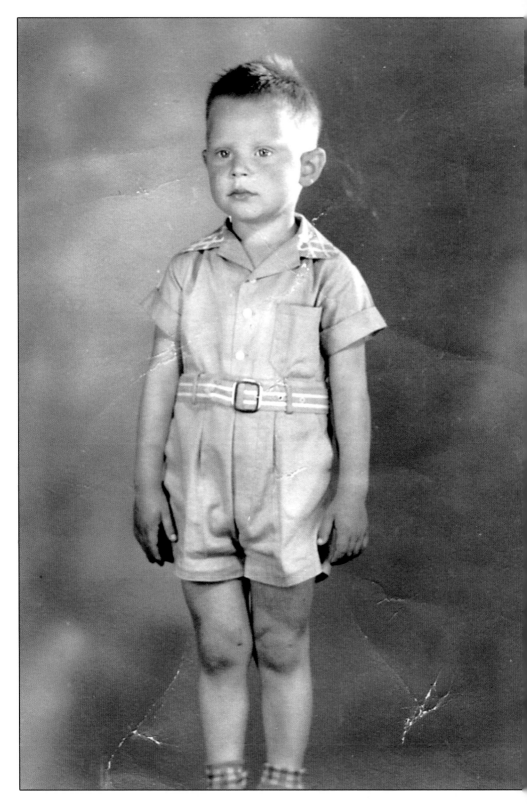

Looking stunned in that same photo shoot!

I'm on the left, with my cousin
Billy McElroy

With my sister Shirley, 1950

My sister Shirley, brother Mike and me on the right.

My sister Shirley holds on for dear life as I take one of my first horse rides.

With my sister Shirley, Nov. 1952

I was dreaming of being Mickey Mantle in July 1955

SCHOOL DAYS 1950-51

LONG CREEK

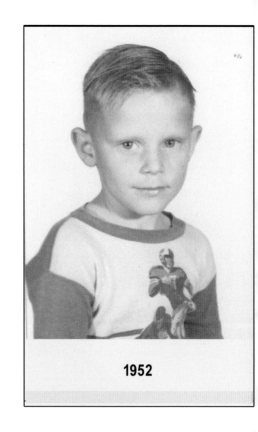

1952

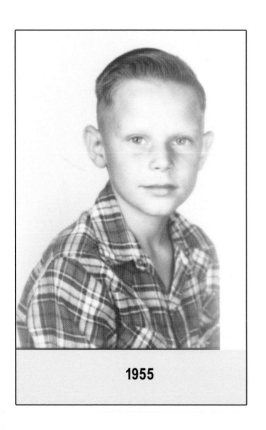

1955

56-57
HOT WELLS JR. HI.

1957

1958

15 years old

High School Graduation

In the middle of my brothers and sister, 1956

With my sister Shirley and my dear friend Frenchy on right, Aug. 1959

Feeding my daughter Laura, 1964

One of my first paying gigs...a Polish wedding!

Courtesy T. Mack-Reynolds Studio

Moe on far right, leads The Mavericks. Our drummer Pete Oellers is smiling big on the far left.

1966 promo photo.
I'm in the middle in the back.

A very thin Moe Bandy and The Mavericks

The Mavericks, 1966.
I'm in the vest.

They always said that we knocked 'em dead

Moe Bandy and The Mavericks. We lost the wagon.

SOUTHWEST ATTRACTIONS
P.O. 20204
San Antonio, Texas 78220

512-653-2476

MOE BANDY

SHANNON RECORDS

1971 Promo Photo.

Singing with the
Johnny Bush
Band, 1970

One of my first
tour buses

With my producer
Ray Baker and
Wesley Rose

The wife of my producer Ray Baker played a
model in this promo shot.

In the studio with The Jordanaires, April 1972, The Jordanaires sang on a
lot of my first records.

An early promo photo

I couldn't believe I was in the same studio as my heroes Roy Acuff and Ernest Tubb.

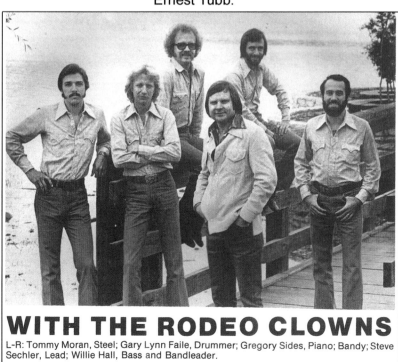

WITH THE RODEO CLOWNS

L-R: Tommy Moran, Steel; Gary Lynn Faile, Drummer; Gregory Sides, Piano; Bandy; Steve Sechler, Lead; Willie Hall, Bass and Bandleader.

My great band. We put a lot of miles on the bus.

Never without my guitar

One of my more unqiue stage outfits

Playing at the Simonton Texas rodeo

Photo courtesy of Betty Urbanek

Bandy The Rodeo Clown

He saved my life in Cheyenne

Dinner with Miss Rodeo USA 1977 and Charley Pride

The Moe Bandy Rodeo Clowns softball team in San Antonio

The plane I had to lease to make it to a show on time.

High flyin' with my band and our own stewardess.

Taking my son Ronnie to visit the
dugout of The Los Angeles Dodgers

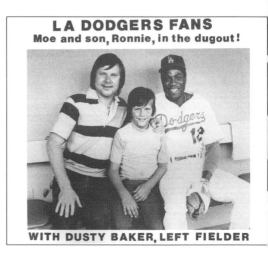

LA DODGERS FANS
Moe and son, Ronnie, in the dugout!

WITH DUSTY BAKER, LEFT FIELDER

Another one for the
trophy case

Moe Bandy

A 1978 tour program

MOE BANDY

Southwest Attractions
"COUNTRY'S BEST"
P. O. Box 20204
San Antonio, Texas 78220
512-653-2476

Can you believe people actually bought this 8 x 10

Making the cover of Nashville West magazine

General Recording Corporation

Atlanta, Georgia

MOE BANDY

t.b.

TOP BILLING, INC.
P.O. Box 12514
Nashville, Tn. 37212
(615) 383-8883

MOE BANDY

Exclusive Bookings

United Talent, Inc.

P.O. BOX 22470 • 1707 DIVISION STREET • NASHVILLE, TENNESSEE 37203 (615) 244-9412

An award-winning album cover

MOE BANDY IN CONCERT

This photo with TG Sheppard ran in Country Song Roundup

time. And I was thrilled when Wally called to ask me to sign with the new label. I was even more elated when 'I Just Started Hatin' Cheatin' Songs Today' ended up at #17 on the national charts!

My second release for GRC, 'Honky Tonk Amnesia', went almost as far, as it landed at #24. I was finally on my way to being a "real" country music artist! That was the good news. But the bad news was… I was so busted, I couldn't even go out on the road to promote my songs. I didn't have enough money to even go out of town to do a show!

When they found out that I was broke, a friend said, "You need to call your record label and have them give you an advance." So I flew to Atlanta to meet with the owner of the label, and when I walked in, there was a bunch of guys sitting around a big table. The president of the company said, "I would like to loan you $5,000." Gratefully, I said, "Man, that would be great. That will sure help me get started."

Then he said, "But you might want to do a little something for me."

I naively replied, "Sure, what can I do for you?" to which the owner said, "Well, we'd like to manage you. And I would like the publishing on your songs. And we'd like you to split up your writing royalties a little and let us in on that."

I looked at him, and noticed that it looked like he was sitting on a little throne. He was the king there. Then it dawned on me that something didn't feel right about the entire deal. I said, "No, I can't do that deal. I'm sorry." I ended up going to Nashville and borrowing the money that I needed.

I had my first top ten song with "It Was Always So Easy to Find an Unhappy Woman." That was followed by "Don't Anyone Make Love at Home Anymore", which came close to the top ten. And then I really hit with the monster, "Bandy the Rodeo Clown." Those hits came in spite of the fact that I had been asking to be released by GRC. I finally had to take them to court in order to get out of my contract.

Later, I found out that the man who'd owned the record label was also in the porno business! A news article came out that called him "The Sultan of Smut." The FBI estimated that he had made more than $100 million in the X-Rated industry before he started GRC Records. With that much money involved, there was also a lot of stuff going on with the mafia. And the head of the record label was accused of killing a guy! He ended up being convicted on charges of arson and pornography distribution, and was sentenced to eight years in prison.

At that time, I thought, "Wow, I said no to that guy. I'm pretty lucky they got him." And guess what... in 1978, he escaped from prison and they couldn't find him! While he was out, he managed to find the man who had accused him of murder... and he killed him and another man!

I was a little worried, but I knew that he had much bigger problems than a little country singer. After the police finally found him again, in 1980 he was convicted on murder charges and sentenced to life in prison. He died in prison in 2013. You would think there would be a great country song in all of that.

THE SAVIOR OF COUNTRY MUSIC

"Moe Bandy is the Jesus Christ of Country Music." Wow. As I read those words in a feature article and review, I really had no idea what they meant… but I thought that it had to be good! Unfortunately, I sure wasn't anything like Jesus Christ.

♫

They say that timing is everything. And it really is. I think you can be the greatest singer in the world, but if the timing isn't right, you might not ever get heard by anyone.

The early 1970s was a time when country music was changing. There were a lot of strings, and a pop sound on most of the records that were coming out of Nashville. Eddy Arnold and Ray Price were having one hit after another, but most of their songs had more of a pop violin than a country fiddle sound.

But then I came along, and I was real country. I was different. And that seemed to work in my favor. All of a sudden this pure, traditional country singer comes out. And it was just perfect timing for someone who was a little different.

A guy named Nick Tosches wrote in The Village Voice that "Moe Bandy is the Jesus Christ of Country Music." I had to ask someone what that meant, and they said, "He is saying you are the savior of country music!" They said that I was changing the music, and getting it back to where it should be.

The next thing I knew, I was out on the road, opening for all of my heroes. It was unbelievable! I was scared to death. I was in a dream world. I had never traveled before. Before I left GRC, Ann Tant was in charge of my publicity, and we would do promotional tours. We'd go to every radio station in the country. We did all the midnight radio shows and all the overnight trucker shows. And I played concerts in between my radio appearances.

One of my first national television appearances came in 1975, when I sang on the popular "Pop Goes the Country" show. It was filmed at the

Opry House. I took my wife and two children with me. My son Ronnie was eleven years old. After the taping, we couldn't find him anywhere. We looked and looked. I was panicking, when I went outside and saw Ronnie sitting on the steps and talking with Roy Acuff. Mr. Acuff was just sitting there, visiting with my little boy.

People in Texas love to dance to live music. You know that a band is really good if everyone is out on the dance floor. I learned to play in South Texas, and you had to play dance music. Dancing is so important to people in South Texas. Lots of times, you would hear about these big name acts, big stars who'd played Texas and the audience would complain and say, "We couldn't even dance to it!"

I've always said if you took a Texan and tied him to a chair while the band played the 'Cotton Eyed Joe', the guy would get hurt trying to get out of that chair so he could dance. He would become Houdini! People in Texas have got to dance.

But once I had some hits and became a 'star', I saw that people had stopped dancing and were watching us sing. That was good for my ego, but it also caused some problems. I would be singing one of my songs, and the crowd would be standing up near the stage watching us, and there would always be some idiot who would dance right through the middle of the crowd. And that's when the fights would start! He'd be dancing, and come right through the people who were watching the show, and it would always end with a big fight. And I would just keep right on singin'.

I learned how to deal with fights that broke out during our show, and I also learned how to mix my songs up so that my show had the best pacing. I learned when to play a waltz, and when to play an up-tempo song. I learned what the folks danced to the most. And I learned how to deal with people coming up and making stupid requests. I learned how to deal with drunks. I learned all that in the beer joints.

One night, I was onstage, and a guy danced up by me and yelled, "Desperado!" Then he made another lap around and again yelled, "Desperado!" When he circled by the third time, when he yelled the same thing, I yelled back, "I don't know Desperado. That's not my song!"

A few years ago, I was talking to a younger singer. He was trying to make it, and his management had sent him to get voice lessons. He also said he couldn't be around smoke at all and before his show, he would not talk for two hours, so that he would save his voice.

I told him, "You should probably find something else to do." I told him to fire his management and go find the smokiest beer joint and the wildest place he could find, and then go play there six nights a week. That is where you get your education.

Nowadays, they are making the artists do all this crap. Today's artists are not getting the same education that we got. Garth Brooks played the beer joints. George Strait played the beer joints. It teaches you how to deal with the people.

They have outlawed smoking in a lot of places now. Of course, I used to smoke myself. But it never bothered me that bad when other people smoked at my shows. I once played a place in Louisiana, it was an old club. My road manager was inside, and I was sitting on our bus, and when he came outside to get me, he opened up the door to the club, and smoke just billowed out. It looked like the place was on fire! That was a rough one. You couldn't even see the people in the first row for all of the cigarette smoke.

Smoke is bad on your throat. Thank God I never had any problems with my voice. I was once doing a show with a new singer, and they were getting ready before they went on. I heard them making this noise with their throat and voice, and I said, "What the hell is that?!"

They said, "I'm warming up."

I said, "It sounded like a damn bird!" I warm up by singing. No bird noises.

♫

I had a big hit with the song, "I Just Threw My Last Bottle at the Jukebox." And we had several people that would throw a bottle at a jukebox, and it would bust the bottle and the jukebox. That happened a bunch. And one time, a guy threw a bottle at me. I was onstage at Schroeder Hall in Texas, when a woman came up to the front of the stage; and she was enjoying the show. Her boyfriend came up, and told her to sit down. When she refused, he threw his beer bottle at me as I was singing. It hit the railing that was above the stage and exploded. Glass got all over my steel player. A couple years ago, I played that same place again, and I told the crowd, "I'm gonna get emotional. This place is special to me. I had my first beer bottle throwed at me right here!"

A few beer bottles also led to my first invitation to appear on the Grand Ole Opry. I was playing in a golf tournament with Faron Young in 1973. He wasn't much of a golfer, but he liked to play. Faron and I won the drinkin' contest at the tournament. We got to drinking, and Faron asked me, "Have you ever been on the Opry?"

I said, "No, I haven't."

He said, "Well, you're gonna be on tonight! I'm gonna bring you on there during my spot."

I was so excited! Later that day, I called my mother so that I could tell her to be sure to tune in to WSM radio. But when she answered, I thought she sounded a little weird. I couldn't wait to tell her, "Mom, I'm going to be on the Grand Ole Opry tonight!" But instead of her being excited, she didn't even comment back to me. Then she whispered, "Your sister had her baby."

I asked her, "Is everything OK?"

Quietly, she said, "We were really concerned about the baby's health. And we found out she has Downs Syndrome." It upset me so much that I called Faron and said, "I better not do the Opry tonight." But that baby turned out to be the greatest blessing our family ever had. I loved her so much back then, and I love her even more today.

A year later, I received an official invitation to be on the Opry. By then, the Opry had moved from the Ryman Auditorium to the new Opry House. The first time I was on, George Morgan introduced me, and I will never forget it as long as I live. When I walked backstage, there was Roy Acuff, Ernest Tubb and Faron Young. I was so scared. It scared me to death to walk out onto that circle of wood that they had cut from the Ryman floor and put onto the new Opry stage.

For my Opry debut, I sang my hits, "I Just Started Hating Cheatin' Songs Today" and "Honky Tonk Amensia." At the time, I was the new traditional country singer. And a lot of the newer artists were going Pop at the time. As I sang, I looked over in the wings, and everyone was watching me, seeing what I could do. I remember Ernest Tubb standing there on the side of stage, and he had a huge smile as he watched me sing. I thought, "Wow! What a thrill."

Today, I play the Grand Ole Opry 3-4 times a year. I'm a lot more relaxed now. I'm more used to it and know what to expect. But there's always a butterfly in your stomach when you walk out onto that circle of wood that they brought from the Ryman. I've heard lots of people talk about the special feeling they get when they stand there. It is always an honor to be on the Opry.

Shortly after my first appearance on the Opry, I was asked to do a radio show in the studio of WSM. And when I got there, I found out that the show was going to be me, Roy Acuff and Ernest Tubb. I didn't think I belonged in the same room with those true legends. But they were both so nice to me.

BANDY

"Moe Bandy saved my life in Cheyenne! He sure did. That was back when he was a rodeo clown. A bull threw me and Moe stepped in and saved my life. Yes, he did."

Those words, or very similar words, have been said so many times over the years. And guess what… there is no truth to them at all!

Let's try to explain this one.

Whitey Shafer wrote my first four hit songs. When I first came to town, I didn't know anybody. But since Whitey was from Waco, Texas, and I was from San Antonio, he ended up taking me around and we palled around together. When he found out that I would cut his songs, he just went to town writing as much as he could. He knew he had an outlet for his tunes.

My brother, Mike, was doing really good in the rodeo in 1974. And I had been having so much success with songs that Whitey Shafer had written, so I called Whitey and I asked him to write me a rodeo song, since my brother was becoming a big rodeo star. A short time later, I got a phone call. When I picked up the phone, the person on the other end said, "Moe, this is Lefty."

I asked, "Lefty who?"

He said, "Lefty Frizzell."

I thought, "Oh my God! One of my heroes is calling me!"

I had met Lefty, just real briefly. I didn't know him that well, but I was such a fan of his. I was awed by Lefty. And here he was, calling me! Lefty said, "We wrote you a rodeo song."

And right then, he and Whitey Shafer sang it to me over the phone.

I told Lefty that I loved the song, and I couldn't wait to get into the studio to cut it. Out of all of the classic country songs Lefty wrote, that song was one of the very last ones he ever wrote, and he wrote it for me.

On December 6, 1974, I walked into Columbia Studio B and recorded "Bandy the Rodeo Clown." And as soon as we'd recorded it, we knew we had a big hit. Everybody was raving about it as we finished the session. It was a different sound for me. It wasn't what I had been doing before.

When I'm recording, I always tell everyone that music is not just hearing. It's feeling. Today, with everything all digital in the studio, you lose that feeling. And when you take the feeling out of the music, when you make the music perfect and you tune every single thing, to me it takes a lot of the heart out of it. But when we recorded "Bandy the Rodeo Clown", we had a feeling that we had a hit record.

"Bandy" turned out to be my signature song. As it was headed up the charts, I got another call from Lefty Frizzell. He was so proud of the song, of me, and I'm sure of himself too. I will never forget how he said, "My boy, you're gonna be a star-ah!" That was one of the last things he ever told me. Lefty died on July 19, 1975. "Bandy" ended up hitting #7 on September 6th. Imagine that… two months after Lefty died, the song that he wrote for me was one of the hottest songs in country music!

To celebrate my huge hit with "Bandy," I wanted to get a new car. Faron Young told me he could get me a great deal on a brand new Lincoln Continental Mark IV. It was beautiful! And it had something that you didn't see much back in 1975… a sunroof! I was so proud of that car that, when I drove it home to Texas, and when I pulled into the driveway, I honked the horn so my family would come running out. When they did, I was driving in, standing up with my head sticking out of that sunroof!

When "Bandy" hit, I played every rodeo in the world. Every weekend, I was at a different rodeo. I would play in the rodeo arena each evening, but during the day, I would hang out with all the cowboys. I was just one of 'em.

So when did I start saving people's lives in the rodeo?

"Bandy the Rodeo Clown" is a great example of when you sing something and it's played on the radio every day, people start to believe it. When I sang over and over, "I'm Bandy the Rodeo Clown", it became a fact in people's minds. People were convinced that I had been a rodeo clown before I got into country music!

Over and over, so many times, I've had people come up to me and say, "You saved my life in Cheyenne, Wyoming!"

They were so sincere. And I'd say, "I wasn't really a rodeo clown."

They'd argue, "Yes, you were!"

I'd finally just go along with them and say, "Well, it was my job and I had to do it." I hated to have the break it to them, to tell them the truth. So sometimes I just went along with it.

I was playing golf one day in Tennessee, and there was a little girl walking toward me. When she got to me, she said, "You saved my daddy's life when he was a bull rider." She was crying. I hugged her and I said, "Honey, it was my job and I was glad to do it." I just couldn't tell her any different.

One time they booked me on a show in Nebraska. When I got there, a guy came out to my bus, and he was dressed as a rodeo clown. He had the whole outfit. And he said, "You rascal!" He had his friends with him, and he turns to them and says, "That's my barrel man right there! He worked the barrel with me." I just stood there.

He said, "I booked you here." I played two shows there, and in between shows, the man set up a table and was demonstrating how to put on clown makeup. I felt so bad, but I thought, "I need to stop this." During my second concert, I told the crowd, "I am sorry. But I was not a rodeo clown. I rode bulls and broncs, but I was never a clown." The guy who booked me was heartbroken. It was a weird deal.

When I thought back to that guy meeting me with "You rascal!", that reminded me of a conversation I once had with Roy Clark. Roy and I were talking about how people will walk up to us and yell, "You rascal you! You remember me? We were in Denver in 1974." And there is no way that we can remember them. So every time Roy sees me, he'll point and say, "You rascal!"

I told that story to Flint Rasmussen. Flint is one of the all-time great bull fighters with the Professional Bull Riders Association. And anytime he sees me, he'll also point at me and say, "You rascal!"

So the next time I come play a show near you, be sure to come up and say, "You rascal you!" and I'll know that you've read my book. Just don't tell me that I saved your dad's life in Cheyenne.

MY LOVE OF RODEO

I had to give up bull ridin' because of my back problem… I had a big yellow streak that ran right down the middle of my back! I also developed stomach problems… I had not guts!

I might not have been a rodeo clown, but I *have* been involved with rodeo for my entire life. I was never a rodeo star, but rodeo has been one of the most important things in my life.

I want to say this right off the bat: all the guys and gals who do rodeo are great athletes. It takes a heck of an athlete to do what they do. Over the years, I've gotten to know all the rodeo cowboys and cowgirls. I got to be very good friends with so many rodeo people. In 2016, my brother and I won an award at the PRCA. It was for families who have been involved in rodeo. In 2007, Mike and I were both honored to be inducted into the Texas Rodeo Cowboy Hall of Fame.

The PRCA, the full rodeo and the PBR have been so good to me over the years. Cody Lambert, the Vice President and Livestock Director for the PBR, is one of my best friends. I knew Cody back when he was riding. He is one of the great cowboys, and he also invented the vest that protects the bull riders. I've become very close friends with him. Cody has been so good to me over the years. He has a big rodeo arena at his house. We have a lot of fun there. I go to his house sometimes and I take my whole band with me. We get a bunch of the cowboys together and have a big time. Sean Gleason, who is the head of the PBR, is also a great friend. I am honored to know Sean. Justin McBride is one of the greatest bull riders in the history of the sport. He is a two time world champion. Justin is a dear friend of mine. He is also a very good singer. But he is kind of shy about it. He always says that he will sing after I sing all of my hits. But after about two hours, he gets the nerve up and he sings great. And Larry Mahan also gets up and sings with me. We have a big jam session with the cowboys.

I got to know a lot of the rodeo cowboys because of my mother's cooking. My mom was a great cook. She and my grandmother were the best cooks in the world. They made the best food. Mom made the best fried chicken. And she made butter beans and great vegetables. My mother loved to cook, and loved to have as many people as possible at each meal.

We always liked to have a lot of people over to our house. And when the big rodeo was held in San Antonio, all the cowboys would come stay at our house. Anytime they could get a free room, they would be there. We had a big room upstairs, and there would be cowboys laying all across the floor in that room as they spent the night. And they couldn't wait to eat a meal that my mother cooked. They still talk about those meals today.

One night, one of those cowboys came into our house drunk. Big Mama, my grandmother from Mississippi, was visiting us at the time as well. She was already in bed, asleep. She was in her 80s. The drunk cowboy climbed in bed with grandma, and you could hear her scream all the way down the block!

Walt Garrison has been a friend of mine for years. I love Walt. He was with the Dallas Cowboys, and he really was Mr. Texas. Everybody loved Walt. I had the honor of meeting him, and then I found out that he was a big fan of my music. And he ended up becoming one of my best friends.

One night I played at the rodeo in Del Rio, Texas, and when I got back to the hotel, I found Walt and a bunch of cowboys throwing each other into the swimming pool... with all of their clothes on. I was wearing a brand new pair of Tony Lama boots, and as I walked through, Walt grabbed me. I started trying to fight him off, screaming, "No! No! I've got brand new boots on!"

Walt just laughed as he threw me in. When I got out of the pool, we all ganged up on Walt and tried to throw him in. But there was no way. He was too strong and he fought us all off.

As we were tussling and yelling, the hotel manager came out and told us we were making too much noise and had to quiet down. As I glanced over at Walt, I knew exactly what was going to happen next. Walt grabbed the manager and threw him right in the pool. They ended up calling the police on us. But the sad thing about that story is this... the very next morning, the hotel manager who we threw in the pool was flying on a plane, when it crashed and killed him.

There are rowdy country music stars who have done some crazy things. But any country star is not in the same league as the rodeo stars who do crazy stuff. The cowboys are rowdy. And one of the rowdiest was my brother Mike. I never made it big in the rodeo, but Mike did. Mike would go on to become one of the biggest stars in rodeo, and looking back at how he started, I know that his life story is as impressive, or even more impressive than mine has been.

When Mike was thirteen years old, my brother Rusty dared him to try to ride one of our jersey milk cows. A short time later, a couple guys told my dad that they were bull riders. Our family had some heffers, and dad told the guys, "I bet you can't even ride these heffers."

The two men tried, and each one got bucked off. But my brother Mike was watching and said, "I bet I can ride one!"

My dad said, "Let's see it."

Mike jumped on and just rode it for all it was worth. My dad got so exited! I don't think one of my #1 songs ever excited him as much as Mike did, the day he rode that heffer! The very next week, Dad had us all building a rodeo arena for him.

My brother Rusty was in charge of "Bandy's Arena." He helped build our first bucking chutes out of beer pallets. But our family arena quickly became so popular that people started coming from everywhere to watch the local cowboys try their hand at bull riding, calf roping and bareback riding. We also built a little bandstand, and when the cowboys needed a break, I would sing with my band The Mavericks.

One of our bulls went on to the National Finals in 1972. But there was no doubt who the big star was at "Bandy's Arena." It was my brother Mike. He was just fourteen years old when he rode his first big bull, but by the time he was fifteen, he could beat any man at bull riding. And bull riding was big in Texas and that part of the country. Mike joined the Professional Bull Riders Association at the age of nineteen, and he started winning everything almost as soon as he started.

And if they gave silver belt buckles for crazy, Mike would have a trophy case full. Let me tell you a few stories about my brother.

Mike never wore underwear when he slept. He slept in the nude. He got drunk one night in Cheyenne. And he was so drunk that when he got back to his hotel, he didn't realize he wasn't in his room. Nope, he had only made it as far as the hotel lobby! And right there in the lobby, Mike took off all his clothes, everything, and he laid down on the couch and went to sleep! The front desk called one of Mike's rodeo friends,

Hooter Brown, to come down. He came and picked Mike up and carried him to his room!

Hooter Brown was a great saddle bronc rider, and one of the toughest guys in the world. Hooter went with Tanya Tucker for several years. Any time Hooter and my brother Mike would get together, you just knew they were going to do something crazy. One night, when they got bored at a bar, they went next door to a firehouse and they stole a fire truck!

Mike was driving the truck, and he and Hooter were both wearing the fire helmets. They wanted to drive the truck over to the bar and fire one of the water hoses into the bar, but he wasn't able to get the truck to stop, and they crashed it into a yard that was next to the bar. Mike and Hooter ran away. But for some reason, Mike ended up calling the Sheriff himself. When the Sheriff answered, Mike said, "You're gonna have to get up mighty early in the mornin' to catch ole Mike Bandy!"

Hooter Brown and fire equipment also played roles in another one of Mike's escapades. There was a room full of people backstage at one of my concerts, and Mike grabbed a fire extinguisher and hosed down everyone in the room. He blew that extinguisher everywhere, including all over an important guy from CBS Records who happened to be there. The guy had white foam all over his hair and eyebrows. When I found out about that, I was so mad.

But that was nothing compared to what my brother did one night in Fort Worth. I was doing a show, and afterward a man came running up, yelling, "That cowboy there ran into my truck!" He was pointing at my brother. Mike just smiled at him and said, "Let me take a look." As soon as I saw the look on his face, I knew Mike was about to do something crazy. And I was right! Mike went up to the truck, unzipped his pants, and started peeing on it! He peed all the way down the entire side of it. Then he zipped up his pants and told the guy, "That's what I think of your damn truck."

Mike would get thrown in jail for getting in brawls. He was banned for life from a bar in Cow Town in Fort Worth. He started a food fight during a wedding there.

Mike once met a gal at a rodeo, who had one of those little overhead campers on her pickup. Mike and her spent the night together in the camper, and the next morning, while he was still asleep, she got into the truck cab and drove off. And she ran right into a low-hanging awning. It just sheered the top off that camper and there stood Mike, wrapped in a sheet, wondering what had happened to him!

Mike rode bulls for more than twenty years. He was only 5 foot 4 inches tall, just a little-bitty guy. But he always thought that he was bigger than a house, and he was. He would try anything. We were out on the town in Fort Worth one night, and as we walked out of a bar, a cop came up to us. The cop was a horse patrol, and he started to ask Mike if he had been drinking too much. And as soon as he did, Mike jumped on the back of the horse! Mike started spurring the horse, and the horse started bucking. The cop was holding on for dear life. I could tell that policeman was irate, and I was trying to help as I yelled, "He's my brother!"

The cop yelled back, "I don't care who he is. I'm going to shoot your brother if he don't get his ass of my horse!"

♫

Dan Mitchell wrote a song called "Rodeo Romeo." As soon as I heard it, I said, "That is my brother. I have to record that." It really fit Mike perfectly. Mike is still one of the funniest guys I have ever been around. He buys and sells cattle now. Since I have talked so much about him, I thought it was only fair to give him a chance to give his side.

♫

"Growing up back then in South Texas was not easy. We had no air conditioning, and most days in the summer the temperature would hit 110 degrees or more. All of us kids slept in bunk beds. And Dad brought in these big blower fans, like you see in hog or cattle barns. He set them up in our bedrooms, and we all tried to sleep in front of those big fans.

But things changed dramatically for the entire Bandy family in the mid 1970s. 1974 was the year that Moe and I both really hit. We both kind of became stars in our profession at just about the same time. But my success came a lot easier and faster than Moe's did. When he was starting out, we all wished him the best. And ten years later, he was still trying to make it, and we were all still cheering him on.

But to be honest, I couldn't really believe that he was able to stick with it for twelve years before he ever had any success! He just stayed with it, when almost anyone else would have quit. He was so dedicated and believed in himself. And he just loved singing and entertaining. Moe was really rejected for twelve years! My success at bull riding came much easier than his music success. I was successful at each level I was at, from the time I started out as a teenager and as I worked my way up.

But even then, our dad still always asked both of us, "When are you boys gonna get a real job?"

But our dad was totally speechless one day in 1974. 'Wide World of Sports' was covering the Denver Nationals. It was the big time. And I ended up winning the darn thing. Curt Gowdy interviewed me for Wide World. After the interview, I called my parents to tell them that I had won, and I said, "Daddy, you won't believe what just happened."

Daddy said, "I don't know how much more I can take." I asked him what he meant, and he said, "Moe just called a little while ago and said that he has signed a recording contract with GRC Records." Both those huge events happened on the same day."

– Mike Bandy, Moe's Brother

♫

Mike loved to ride bulls. And he also liked to sing every now and then. I think when he saw his big brother up on a stage in front of thousands of fans, he thought he could also do the same thing. That thinking might have been altered by some of the alcohol he had been drinking!

When I played different rodeos or a Texas honky-tonk, Mike would sometimes come up onstage and sing harmony with me. Sometimes he'd even sing one or two songs on his own. He wasn't real good, but he was so popular and loved by all the rodeo fans and everyone in Texas that they didn't care. They loved seeing one of their heroes up there trying to sing.

Then Mike came up with this alter ego that he named Rex February. That's his stage name! One New Year's Eve, I found out that 'Rex February' had gotten himself booked at the annex of the huge Billy Bob's club! I went to see the show and Mike... I mean Rex... walked out wearing this long trench coat and sunglasses. The crowd had no idea what was going to happen. And I'm pretty sure that Rex didn't either! But he sure was entertaining.

This past year, when I played the famous Longhorn Saloon in Fort Worth, Texas, Rex February joined me onstage and he stole the show. The place went crazy. He ended up singing a few songs. He would drink a little bit in between each song, and I have to say that the more he drank, the worse he sang!

I have one more favorite childhood memory of Mike... even though it was a day that he would like to forget! When we were kids, our dad gave Mike a haircut. And it was awful. It was the worst haircut in the world. His hair was so notched-up, he looked like a POW.

Mike and my brother Rusty had to feed our hogs every morning. And we would feed them a big bucket of slop. It was made up of left-over, thrown-out food from a local restaurant. It had old bread and table scraps, and we added some milo to it. It was basically just a big bucket of garbage.

So Mike took his bad haircut and the big bucket of slop to the hog pen. Mike had to climb over a fence to get to the hogs. He was very short, and the five-gallon bucket was very heavy. Mike lifted the bucket over his head as he straddled the top of the fence, and right at that moment, he dropped it. And slop went all over his head!

As he climbed down, one of our horses came running over to the fence. The day before, the horse had cut its foot, and Daddy had sprayed it with this medicine called Gentian Violet. It was purple stuff, and if it got on you, it didn't come off. It has to wear off over a week or two.

Just as Mike was starting to wipe the slop off of his head, that horse kicked some of that Gentian Violet and it sprayed all over Mike's face! His face was purple!

Mike and Rusty ran back to the house to try and clean him up, but before they got inside, the school bus was coming down the road. They had to get on.

So there he was. With a horrible haircut. And now, he also had slop in his hair. And his face was purple. Could it get any worse? Yes, it could. When he got to school, Mike found out that it was picture day!

It's hard to believe that poor little boy went on to be one of the all-time rodeo greats. But he did.

My parents were so proud of all their children. All of us were very successful at what we did, and mother always kept the newspaper and magazine clippings about me and Mike. She saved them all. She was so proud.

One of my favorite memories is of the night I sang at the big rodeo at the Houston Astrodome. I performed with Joe Stampley, and we broke the Thursday night record with 45,000 people in attendance. I got my mom and dad box seats so that they had a perfect view of everything. And that night, not only did they get to watch me perform in front of that huge crowd, but they also got to see their son Mike win the bull riding competition. Our parents were so proud. It was a very special night for me and my family.

I am still involved with the rodeo business, now as a bull owner. My brother Rusty and I bought a bull and named it Moebandy.com. It became a really great bull. It also got me a lot of attention. That bull got more TV time than I ever did! But it was crazy to hear the PA announcer say, "Moe Bandy is in shoot three!"

But there is one problem with owning bulls: I found myself sitting in the stands next to the mother or wife of the rider who was trying to stay on the bull. I would be cheering for the bull, and the woman next to me would be cheering for her boy. And when I'm cheering for the bull to buck really great and throw the cowboy, that doesn't go over very well with the mother or wife of the cowboy.

Moebandy.com is retired now. He had a great career. After he retired, we moved him up to Missouri, where I live, and he's enjoyed his later years in the pasture with a bunch of cows.

Since we had so much success with Moebandy.com, Rusty and I bought another one that we named Bandy's Bad Boy. They both came from parents who were great bucking stock. Bandy's Bad Boy is still out there on the main circuit, and is doing real good. We have had a lot of fun following our bulls around the PBR.

Chad Berger has some of the greatest bulls in the PBR. Chad and I became friends. I was doing some shows in England, and I invited Chad and his wife to go with us. We did all the tourist things, and we went to a steakhouse in London. Chad is very country and not used to these ritzy places. He ordered a steak. It was very expensive, and cost about $300. And when they brought him this tiny and very thin piece of meat, Chad cut into it and yelled, "Steak! This ain't a steak!"

HITTING THE BIG TIME

In 1976, I was nominated for Most Promising Male Artist of the Year by the Academy of Country Music. Also up for the award were Rex Allen, Jr., Larry Gatlin, Billy Crash Craddock, and Johnny Lee. And guess who won... Moe Bandy! I'll have to remind Larry and Johnny about that the next time I see them! Johnny won his awards a couple years later after he recorded "Lookin' for Love."

I was thrilled that I had won the award. It was probably the highlight of my career to date. But I have a huge regret about it: I was not there to accept the award. I had a booking that I could not get out of. I tried my best to get out of the date, but the promoter threatened to sue me if I cancelled.

And then I was the very last person to know that I had won the award. I did my concert, but after the show, we couldn't find a hotel room, so we slept on the bus. We didn't have cell phones or the Internet back then, so by the time I went to a pay phone and called my wife, she yelled, "You won the award!"

I had no idea that I was going to win. I should have been there. That was one of the biggest mistakes I've ever made. Dan Water of Columbia Records accepted the award for me. I felt terrible that I wasn't there.

But I was in the right spot at the right time one night in the late 70s. We were driving our tour bus down a small road in rural Georgia, and up ahead, we could see a bunch of smoke. And when we got closer, we realized that someone's house was on fire.

We stopped the bus, and everyone jumped out. We saw the family trying to get their possessions out of the burning house, and we just started running as fast as we could. We helped them save a lot of things before the house totally burned.

When the fire department got there and the family calmed down a little, they started looking at our bus. And none of them could believe who had helped them!

On October 10, 1978, I recorded two of the biggest hits of my career, and I recorded them both on the same day. One was "Barstool Mountain", and the other was "It's a Cheatin' Situation." I did have some second thoughts about doing "Cheatin' Situation", but I really didn't get much flack about the song. Most of my songs were about real life. People do cheat and people do drink. Most of my drinking songs were about people who had problems with drinking. My songs didn't really glorify the drinking, and I never did advocate drinking.

When we did "Cheatin' Situation", we knew we needed a female voice on it, almost like a duet. We tried it with one woman, but it wasn't exactly what we wanted. So we asked Janie Fricke's manager if she would do it. She had a couple hit records at the time, and it was so nice of her to do that for us. She came in and just nailed it. It was just perfect. As soon as we cut the song, we just felt like we had a hit. When you do a lot of songs, you hope they're going to be hits. You know they're good, but you just never know. But with this song, we all knew it would be big.

I did a concert with Janie Fricke in Dallas, Texas in 1989. It was for the employees of Braniff Airlines. Braniff was headquartered at Dallas Love Field. Razzy Bailey was also on the show with me and Janie. And we all got paid in Braniff Airlines tickets!

But just a couple days after the show, Braniff announced it was moving its entire operation to Orlando Florida. And shortly after that move, the company went entirely bankrupt. 10,000 employees lost their jobs, and I lost all of my airplane tickets. When I heard the news about Braniff shutting down, I thought, "Wow, none of those thousands of people who were in our audience had any idea they would be out of work just two days later." It was a sad thing.

Janie and I still do quite a few shows together. She is still one of the best singers ever. She has perfect pitch, and sings so great. It is always a joy to work with her. We are still very good friends. I asked Janie if she wanted to say a few words in my book.

♫

"I was a backup vocalist in the 1970s. I was a studio harmony singer with a group called The Lea Jane Singers. But in 1977, Johnny Duncan featured me on the duet "Come A Little Bit Closer." A year later, I did a hit duet with Charlie Rich called "On My Knees." I was also just beginning to have my first success as a solo artist. And then I got a call from Moe Bandy!

I had not met Moe before we did "Cheatin' Situation." But I was thrilled that he wanted me to sing with him. And that song led me to more duets with Vern Gosdin, Merle Haggard and George Jones. I couldn't believe that I was singing harmony and doing full duets with all these legends.

I have done quite a few shows with Moe over the past couple of years. And the audience really loves it when we sing "Cheatin' Situation" together. It brings back memories for the audience, and it is really fun for me and Moe too. It's hard to believe that 40 years have passed since we recorded that song. And it's amazing when you hear the response of the crowd as soon as Moe starts singing the first words of the song all these years later.

Moe is a workaholic. He loves to work. He does a wonderful show. He is so entertaining. And he has so many hits. It is really incredible. I just love to sit backstage and listen to his show. Off stage, Moe is so nice. He puts everybody in such a good mood. He is a genuinely good person. He is a gentleman and such a great guy.

– Janie Fricke

♫

I took the photo for the "Cheatin' Situation" album cover in December. I had shaved the morning of the photo shoot, but since I had a couple months off for Christmas, I decided to try to grow a beard. I had never had one, and I wanted to see what it would be like while I had the time off. But once I grew it, I never got rid of it.

Today's current stars have to get their clothes and hair and entire image OK'd by consultants, but back then, we did what we wanted. When Conway Twitty got his perm, he didn't get it OK'd by any fashion consultant. And after Conway got his perm, then T.G. Sheppard got his. And then Gene Watson got a perm. I never got one.

♫

I won the ACM award for Song of the Year for "It's a Cheatin' Situation", and I made sure I was at those awards! Curly Putman and Sonny Throckmorton wrote "Cheatin' Situation." The same year, Sonny also wrote "Last Cheater's Waltz" for T.G. Sheppard, and that was also nominated for the same award. Sonny must have had cheatin' on his mind that year! He and Whitey Shafer were the kings of cheating songs.

In 1980 my producer, Ray Baker, was also producing a young gal named Judy Bailey. We ended up recording the duet, "Following the Feeling." And that song made it all the way into the top ten on the charts. Judy was from Kentucky, and she was country. And I mean she was so country that she would make Loretta Lynn look like a city girl! How country was Judy? When we got our hit song, she celebrated by buying her mom and a dad a telephone. They had never had one before! And this was in 1980! To install the phone, Judy's dad cut a hole through the entire wall, so they could answer the phone from the kitchen or from the living room! Judy was a very sweet gal. She was very talented and a very good singer.

My partnership with Ray Baker is probably one of the most successful of any artist/producer in country music. Ray was great for my career. He was responsible for me making it. There is no doubt about that. And I have always said that.

Ray had some success before we got together. He had the great Dallas Frazier writing for him. They had cut some stuff. He also had Whitey Shafer writing for him. And Whitey ended up writing so many of my songs. Doodle Owens was also on Ray's staff, and all those guys just went to work writing songs for me. And they were some of the greatest writers in Nashville!

After I joined up with him, Ray was able to build up two publishing companies. They were worth millions of dollars. He also ended up signing many writers just because he had me. He'd tell them, "If you join my publishing company, you'll get a Moe Bandy cut." That arrangement worked good, as long as I got good songs.

But after a while, we got to cutting songs that were just with Ray's publishing company. I wasn't getting any outside songs to record. If he didn't own the publishing rights, I never saw the song. Finally, the head of CBS records called me in and said, "Either you have to get a new producer and start cutting different material, or we are going to have to let you go."

When I left Ray, he got so mad at me. He stayed mad for years. I finally met up with Ray, and I apologized to him. We met for lunch a few years ago, and we kind of healed everything up. I said, "I am sorry Ray. I have the upmost respect for you and what you did for me." I have to give him credit for everything he did when I was starting out. But now, as I write this book, he is still mad at me.

I also had a falling-out with another longtime friend; Ronnie Spillman was one of the best country music bookers in Texas. He started booking me into different clubs and honky tonks in 1964. That was many years before I had my first hit song.

In 1978, I became part owner with Ronnie in Encore Talent. It was a booking agency. Ronnie was the company President, and Ray Baker was Encore's Vice President.

Almost as soon as we started, Encore Talent became a very successful business. Of course, we were booking me. And I was booked solid. We also booked Johnny Duncan and Red Steagall. They were all very popular, especially around Texas. We also booked Gene Watson. Every date that Gene had back then was booked through our agency.

One day, Red Steagall brought in a little, red-haired gal. He asked if we could try to get her some bookings. We ended up having her open some shows for me, and we also got her some other dates. That gal was Reba McEntire.

But me and Ronnie Spillman had a bad split. It all ended up with a lawsuit, and it was a bad deal. I hate that it ended the way it did.

Reba McEntire happened to be on the bill for one of my most memorable shows.

I was playing a fundraiser in Oklahoma City with Reba and Red Steagall, and my friend Mike Hudson, who we all called Hud, was visiting me on my bus before the show. I jokingly asked him, "Hud, how about you coming on stage and singing harmony with me on 'Here I Am Drunk Again'?"

Excitedly, Hud said, "Sure! I'd love to! What should I wear?"

I said, "Just grab something from my closet back there." As Hud walked toward the back of the bus, I grabbed my guitar and left to start my show.

You have to remember that the country stars were wearing different clothes back then. At the time, I was wearing these big, heavy jumpsuits. They were like Elvis used to wear. And while I was onstage singing, I had no idea that ol' Hud was on my bus trying to squeeze into one of my very best jumpsuits!

When I started in on "Here I am Drunk Again", I said to the crowd, "And now, I want to introduce my friend from Nashville, Tennessee…" Here came Hud, and he was wearing one of my best, most expensive Nudie suits! It was covered in rhinestones, with one of those big Elvis collars. And it had a huge horse that covered one side of the outfit.

Hud could barely zip the suit up, and he was wearing huge sunglasses. The audience was trying to figure out who he was… and so was I! My band just fell over when he came out. And when he got back to the bus, he could barely get that suit off.

Hud was working for the Coors beer company at the time. He ran their pro rodeo program, and he always kept me and my band stocked up with beer. One time in Sikeston, Missouri, he put a bunch of beer on the bus. He gave us ten cases. The next week, I called him and said, "Don't you ever put ten cases of beer on my bus! My band was drunk for four days! They could barely play!"

♫

"I shared an apartment in Dallas with Moe's brother Mike. And I have been close friends with Moe ever since. From the time I was introduced to him, he has always been like a brother to me. He has always been a great friend. Anything that he could do for me, he would. He has never turned anyone down. If he could help them in any way, he was there. He has always been a great guy, and an upstanding man. I think the world of him."

- Mike "Hud" Hudson

♫

When a country music star rolls into town, all the fans think, "Wow, what a glamorous life they have. Traveling in that big, fancy bus. That is really the life." Well, I hate to burst your bubble, but our life isn't as glamorous as you might think. And that big, fancy bus? I've probably cussed it more than anything I own. I have gone through 8-10 buses in my career, most of them I bought brand new. But it doesn't matter if you have a brand new bus or a used one, they will all break down.

I don't know anyone who owns a bus who doesn't have problems with them. There are too many moving parts in them, and one of those is bound to stop at any time. Over the years, I've had to rent cars and vans, U-Haul trailers, anything to get us to our next show on time.

One of my most memorable trips was to California. We had played a show at Disneyland, and were headed to San Jose. I had an old 1954 GMC Coach bus that had seen better days. We were driving down the Interstate when we saw police lights flashing in our rearview mirror. And when we pulled over, I could tell the highway patrolman was not in a happy mood. He was also covered with something black all over his uniform.

He asked, "Who owns this bus?"

"I do," I said.

He said, "Step out of the bus and come back here a minute." He walked me to the back of the bus, and then he pointed back at his police car. His entire windshield was covered with oil! We had blown an engine, and it was blowing out oil all over the cars behind us. And when the cop started following us, his car got covered! To make things even worse, he had been using his windshield wipers to see through the oil. And when he pulled us over and got out of his car, he kept his wipers going, and they splattered that oil all over the front of his uniform! He said, "You park that damn bus and don't move it from right there."

We weren't far from San Jose and when the cop drove away, I told our driver, "Let 'er eat boys. We're going to San Jose!" He fired the bus up, and we went into San Jose smoking.

We left our bus in San Jose to get fixed while we headed to our next show. That concert was in New Mexico, so we rented a U-Haul truck and trailer. We loaded all of our instruments and gear from the bus onto it, and took off. After the concert, we came back out and the U-Haul and trailer were both gone. Someone had stole it. Luckily we had our instruments with us on stage. But all the cases and other equipment that was inside the U-Haul were gone. They never did find it.

And here's one more story about those glamorous tour buses… we did a cruise in Florida, Johnny Lee and Lane Brody were also there. Me and my band were going to drive all night so that we could meet the ship. And we had made it all the way to the entrance of the ship dock parking lot, when our bus completely died. It stopped and wouldn't go another inch. We were at the parking lot, but it was a huge lot, and we had a long way to go.

I looked out the window, and I could see the ship I was supposed to be on. The band all jumped out and started pushing the bus. As we pushed it closer to the ship, I could hear yelling and laughing. I looked over, and I saw Johnny Lee on the rail of the ship. He was watching us and just laughing his head off.

MOE AND JOE

In August of 1981, the Texas legislature passed a resolution proclaiming Moe Bandy "The King of Honky Tonk Music." My friend, Senator Peyton McKnight, presented me with the honor. In my acceptance speech, I said, "I'm not sure what The King of Honky Tonk Music does, but I'll try to uphold my reputation!" When I made that joke, I could never have dreamed that just a year later, "The King" would soon be dressing like a Queen! Here's the story of Moe and Joe.

♫

I was booked to play the Wembley Festival in London, England in 1978. It's one of those big concerts with a bunch of acts, and one of those other acts was Joe Stampley. Joe was racking up some impressive hit songs, including the #1s "Soul Song", "Roll On Big Mama", and "All These Things."

Joe and I got into a crap game while we were on the plane on the way to England. During the game, he looked up at me and he asked, "Anybody ever tell you that we look alike?"

I laughed and said back, "Hell, I hope not!"

That night, Joe invited me to meet him for supper at the Hard Rock Café in London. And while we were eating, he said, "Moe and Joe. That sounds like Waylon and Willie. It has a ring to it. We ought to cut something together." The combination of Moe and Joe was all Joe Stampley's idea.

Ansley Fleetwood, Joe's piano player and band leader, was also there, and he was listening to our conversation. A short time later, Ansley came to me and said, "I wrote that song."

"What song?" I asked.

He said, "That song that you and Joe could cut. It's called 'Just Good Ol' Boys'." He played it for me. I liked it, but I said that it needed a chorus. So he went back and wrote the "Other than a wild hair once in a while" chorus. And that really made the song.

I had a recording session, and I had a little time left at the end, so we brought Joe in and we recorded the song. Joe tells the story a different way, but that's the way it happened. The Moe and Joe stuff was really just an experiment. We didn't know if it would work. We were just playing around to see what would happen.

When we finished the record, we took it to the record label, and when they heard "Just Good Ol' Boys" they just went nuts! It wiped them out. They started talking about all the promotion and press ideas they had with the "Good Ol' Boys" theme. They put the song out, and the entire record company really got behind it. And it went straight to #1! As a matter of fact, the first three songs Joe and I sang together all went to the top of the charts. "Holding the Bag" ended up in the top ten, and "Tell Ole I Ain't Here, He'd Better Get on Home" was also a big hit.

We starting touring as 'Moe and Joe', and we did concerts all the way from the east coast to the west coast. We were on the road for months. And the good ol' boys came out of the woodwork as they packed every show that we did! We also met a lot of wild, good ol' girls! We partied every night. We partied onstage every night, and then we partied even harder when we got offstage.

Ansley Fleetwood, the man who wrote "Good Ol' Boys", got drunk one night. He was so drunk that he staggered up to my band and said, "Anybody who can pee in my pocket without smilin', I'll give 'em a hundred dollars!" We all looked at him. And again he said, "If you can pee in my pocket and not smile, I will give you a hundred dollars." I have no idea what he was thinking.

Bill Bowers, who played bass for me, had about two six-packs in him, and he went up to Ansley and he said, "I'll take you up on that!"

So we all went outside and watched as Bill started peeing in Ansley's pocket! Bill stood there peeing, and never once cracked a smile. The pee was going down Ansley's leg and going into the street. When it was over, Ansley gave him the one hundred dollars. Right then, Joe Stampley walked out and yelled, "What the hell is goin' on?! Ansley, you ain't getting on my bus with piss all over your pants! You get a cab!" Poor Ansley lost a hundred dollars and then had to pay for a ride back to his room… not to mention the pee all over his pants!

Joe and I ended up having a half-dozen big hit songs. We had three albums, and our "Good Ol' Boys" album went gold. One of the big hits we had came thanks to Conway Twitty. I was on a plane with him, and he told me, "Y'all ought to go back and get that old Carl Smith song, 'Hey Joe'." Conway was one of the best song pickers in the world. He knew how to pick songs that would be hits, not only for himself, but also for other artists. He helped so many artists with his advice on what songs they should do, and Joe and I ended up recording 'Hey Joe', which turned out to be a huge hit for us.

'Moe and Joe' became one of the hottest acts in country music. Joe and I won the Country Music Association Vocal Duo of the Year award in 1979. And guess who they had present us with the award… Zsa Zsa Gabor and Bobby Bare! What a combination of total opposites! I'm sure that it was the only time in her life that Zsa Zsa ever said the words, "Moe Bandy." When me and Joe ran up to get our award, Zsa Zsa probably had no idea who these two rednecks were! When she handed the award to Joe, he told her, "God love ya!" A year later, we won the Academy of Country Music's Top Vocal Duet award.

The Moe and Joe act got so popular that we had a nightclub with our name on it. The Gilley's club in Texas had become super popular after the movie "Urban Cowboy" came out, and we had an investor who wanted us to open a Moe and Joe's Club. It was north of Houston in Spring, Texas.

We opened the club, and it did really good. While the Gilley's club had the popular mechanical bucking bull, our club had a bucking armadillo! And someone wrote in to the TV show 'You Asked For It' and asked them to get me to ride the armadillo. So the TV show came in one night at about 1:00 am, and they had a film crew that filmed me riding that damn armadillo until daylight! I could barely walk the next day.

We had a lot of the Houston Oilers players come out to the club, too. And Moe and Joe's did so well that they opened a second club in Bossier City, Louisiana, which was only fifty miles from Joe's hometown of Springhill. But it didn't do that well.

Joe and I never owned the clubs; they just paid us to use our names. Joe and I worked the clubs individually, and we also worked them together sometimes. And they had other acts that came in when we weren't there. The clubs only lasted a couple years, but they were a fun deal for a while.

The wildest concert that I ever did was a 'Moe and Joe' show in Dallas. It was during a professional wrestling event called Wrestlingthon. We were in the middle of our "Good Ol' Boys" tour, and the good ol' boys and good ole girls came out by the thousands! A couple women threw their brassieres up on stage. We ignored most of those... but all of the sudden, we looked up and this big ol' pair of underwear came flying up. And the panties were two feet wide! I could see them floating up toward us. When they landed on the stage, Joe picked them up and yelled, "What the hell is this?!"

Joe came to me one day and said, "My boy co-wrote a song. Would you listen to it?"

I said, "Of course I will. If your son wrote it and it's any good, we'll cut it." It turned out to be "Where's the Dress."

As soon as I heard it, I told Joe, "I'll tell you right now, I ain't wearin' no dress. Let's get that straight. I can see that comin' and I ain't gonna do it!" Of course, a short time later, we were in our dressing room, putting on our dresses!

When we cut "Where's the Dress", I didn't have a clue who Boy George was. He didn't play much in Texas! But the song was a parody of Boy George, who was really huge in the pop music world. Boy George wore women's makeup and dresses. He was pretty far out there, at least at the time. But compared to what is going on today, he was fairly tame.

After we recorded the song, the record label wanted us to do a photo shoot to promote it. They had these crazy outfits. I looked at them and I shouted, "Look, I told you before we started that I was not going to wear a dress!" Right then, Joe walked in and already had his dress on! I laughed so hard that I fell on the floor. I said, "Man, if you're going to do that, I guess I can too." They immediately handed me my dress. They had it ready to go. And they wanted to get me in it before I backed out.

We made a music video for the song with Jim Owens. We spent $15,000 on that video. Roy Acuff agreed to be in it with us, and in the video, he runs us off of the Grand Ole Opry stage with his fiddle bow! He had no idea what we were doing, but he went along with everything we asked. When he saw me in my dress, he said, "I don't know what you boys are doin', but I hope you make some money at it."

Filming the video was fun. We did some crazy stuff in it. We filmed a lot of it out at the park by Vanderbilt in Nashville. And there were

Practicing my best smile

On tour with my son Ronnie in 1980.

My brother Mike presenting me with the Lone Star Circuit Entertainer of the Year Award. *Photo courtesy, Jerry Lackey*

My brother Mike at the 1982 National Finals Rodeo. No*tice the very appropriate sign right above his head!*

With my dad and brother Mike. Courtesy Rick Henson

With my family at a show. Lynn, Rusty, Shirley, John, Me, Jimmy, Mom, Dad, Mike. Courtesy Rick Henson

My brother Mike showing how easy it is to be a champion bull rider.

All of the Bandy Boys. (L-R) John, Mike, Dad, Me, Rusty, Jimmy

Celebrating my 35th birthday

Singing at Gilley's

As I sing 'Hank WIlliams You Wrote My Life', Hank looks over my shoulder.

An early photo of me and Gene Watson. Either I am not thrilled with what he's saying, or I am drunk...Probably both!

(Left to Right) Darrell McCall, Red Steagall, Me, Hank Cochran, Darrell Royal, Dad. Courtesy Rick Henson

Standing proudly in front of my tour bus.

I could have been anohter Weird Al, but I decided to keep my guitar!

I'm playing a toy guitar while my drummer Gary Faile tries out a toy drum

One last photo before we go on the road again.

MOE BANDY

"ON BARSTOOL MOUNTAIN"

The Champ at the height of my drinking

With Best wishes (& Thanks!) to Mr. Dandy

Jimmy Carter

President Jimmy Carter asked me to pose for this photo!
Billy Bob is on the far right.

Another night, another stage

On stage with Judy Bailey

Freddy Fender and my daughter Laura on our two week
Europeon Tour.

With all of my band and crew on our European tour.

With Floyd Tillman and Razzy Bailey

Johnny Paycheck, Me, Ricky Skaggs, Ronnie McDowell, Joe Stampley and
Buddy Killen

I had some unique hair going this night.

MOE BANDY

Always happy to pose for a photo

Photo courtesy of Betty Urbanek

All dressed up and ready to party!

Becky Hobbs and
[p]erform our hit duet.

*Photo courtesy,
Linda Martin*

[ ] casual stage outfit

On the road with my family.

One of my more dressier stage outfits

My buddy Gene Watson back when he permed his hair!

Legendary football coach Bum Phillips. Courtesy Stan Denny, Courier-Journal and Louisville Times

Kenny Stabler. Courtesy Stan Denny,
Courier-Journal and Louisville Times

On the field with coach Bum Phillips and Earl Campbell.
Courtesy Courier-Journal and Louisville Times

Souvenir Program

Love you
Moe Bandy

Moe Bandy

An autographed tour program

With George Strait.
Courtesy Rick Henson

Moe with Coach Darrell Royal

On the bus with
my son Ronnie.

Golfing with Willie
Nelson and
Lee Trevino, Feb. 1983

Lake Tahoe
with Willie Nelson

Golfing with
Lee Trevino and
Willie Nelson

March 5 1987

Leroy   Joe   George   Moe   Gary   Ronnie
Urbanek Stampley Strait   Bandy   Morris   Spillman

My family (L-R) Mark, Laura's husband, Laura, my ex-wife
Margaret, Me, Ronnie. My daughter Lisa in the front.

An autographed photo from Ralph Emery. The photo shows
Ralph, my mom and dad, me and Johnny Rodriguez.

Moe Bandy

CBS Records

For Exclusive Bookings Contact:
Ronnie Spillman

Encore
Talent inc.

2137 Zercher Rd.
San Antonio, Texas 78209
512/822-2655

"Top Name Entertainment"

Early 80's promo photo

Moe, Bubba Littrel, George Strait and Johnny Bush.
Courtesy of Rick Henson

In the Macy's
Thanksgiiving Day Parade
I'm on the top left.

*Courtesy of
J. Vance Buitendorp*

Moe and Joe - The Good Ole Boys

My brothers Mike and
Jimmy backstage with
me and Joe Stampley

Ricky Skaggs drops in on
Moe and Joe in this photo
from the early 80's.

Kenny Stabler singing
with Moe and Joe

Football great Kenny Stabler in front of the
Moe & Joe's Club

Comedy legend Carol Burnett visits Moe & Joe

Joe, Hank Thompson and me.

Joe Namath meets Moe and Joe

Joe Stampley and I promote our song "Where's The Dress" on the Music City News Awards.

With Joe Stampley at Billy Bob's, Fort Worth Texas. March 1999.
Courtesy Charles E. Wilkins

Presenting an ACM Award with Shelly West. *Courtesy Neil Pond*

Jan Howard, Lee Roy Parnell, Tanya Tucker and Moe

One of my last photos with Coach Bum Phillips, shortly before he passed away.

Visiting with Randy Travis and his wife Mary

Recording with The Oak Ridge Boys and Jimmy Capps

Enjoying a laugh with Bill Anderson

Doing a special Veteran's Day show with Colonel Oliver North

Singing Cheatin' Situation with Janie Fricke

Buying a plane with my buddy Gus Arrendale

With my friend
Leroy Van Dyke
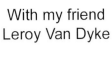

My pals Aaron
Tippin and Mickey
Gilley

With Michele
Capps, my old
girlfriend
Nadine and
Keith Bilbrey

Having a big laugh with the great Ronnie Milsap

My current band. (L-R) Dennis Casey, John Clark, Nick Ochoa, Buster Sharp, Tommy Rials

Debbie and Carrie Moore, Rhonda Vincent, Jett Williams, Razzy Bailey.
Courtesy of Jerry Overcast

Lots of laughs with Darrin Vincent and Johnny Lee

My dear friends Gus Arrendale and T.G. Sheppard

Alaska cruise with Jimmy Fortune, Gene Watson and
Jeannie Seely

some gay guys out there on a boat. Joe was in his dress, and he yelled out to those guys in this gay voice, "You boys get in here real quick!" They were good sports. But I was tryin' to hide, saying, "Please Joe, get back in the truck."

We drove from Opryland to that park in a Winnebago. I was hiding inside, but Joe took his own truck. And he stopped to get gas while he was wearing that outfit! He's out pumping his gas, wearing that dress, and everybody was honkin'.

The video ended up becoming so popular that it was nominated for Video of the Year at the American Music Awards in Hollywood. This was not just a country music show; it was every kind of music. We sat next to Rod Stewart, and James Brown, and all of these rockers. When we walked in that night, no one had a clue of who we were. But after Joe and I won the award, everyone was coming up to us saying, "Hey man! Congratulations! You are great!"

As soon as we put the song out, it became a smash. We were getting all kinds of national media attention. Then, all the fun came to a screeching halt... Boy George sued us! He sued us because we'd used the same intro that he had used on his hit song "Karma Chameleon." I said, "I am not paying him any money because I don't even know who Boy George is, and I had nothing to do with putting that intro on it." Joe was the one who had produced the song, along with Blake Mevis. They were the ones who'd added the intro to the record. So they were the ones who ended up paying Boy George $50,000.

Joe and Blake could have probably fought Boy George in court, but they decided not to. That was because Boy George was on an off brand label, but it was really Columbia records. We were also on Columbia, and they wanted us to settle the case. Besides paying the fifty grand, they also had to go back and change the intro to the song. They took off the music that was the same as the Boy George song. The new version sounded totally different. But you can still find the original version out there.

After all these years, I have still never met Boy George. He still doesn't come to Texas much! Joe and I had a show in England, and the tabloids were all running stories about how Boy George was going to run us offstage and out of his country. But he never showed up.

When I look back on "Where's the Dress", I can honestly say that I have regretted doing the song ever since I first heard it. I hated that song! And that's all I heard for a long time; any time someone passed me on the street, they'd yell, "Where's the dress?!" It got very old, very fast. So I bet you are asking, "Where is the dress… that you wore in the video?"

I'm glad you asked… not really. But I'll answer it. I actually took my dress outfit from the video, and threw it in the trash. And then Joe went and got it out. He's still got it.

Let me talk a little about Joe Stampley. Joe and I had some great success together. We sold a lot of records, and played to a lot of sold out crowds. But our time touring together was not always smooth. We are two completely different personalities. I am very laidback, and Joe is a very hyper guy. He is always goin' 90 miles an hour. Back then, everyone thought that Joe was drunk and on drugs. But I was the one who was drunk. Joe was sober! He didn't even hardly drink. He would drink two beers, while I was drinking everything I could find.

The Moe and Joe act was huge. It's hard to describe how hot we were for a couple years. But Moe and Joe as a *duo* almost killed Moe and Joe as solo artists. I know I worked too hard on my individual career, and I think Joe did too, to have all of that work overshadowed by this novelty duo act we had become. I was also not a big fan of the novelty songs that we did, so I made the decision to kill Moe and Joe.

Joe is still a dear friend of mine. I love Joe. But it got to where I was half an act. And I didn't want to be part of a duo. I hated it when someone would book me for a concert, and when I showed up, some people felt like they were only getting half a show because Joe wasn't there. I couldn't go anywhere without hearing, "Where's Joe?", or "Why didn't you bring Joe with you?"

Yeah, that got really old, really fast. That's why I started backing away from it. It's nothing against Joe at all.

Moe and Joe was really good for both of us. We did a big cruise together in 2017. But when we do one show, people get excited and say, "Oh, you guys are back together again!" So while I will still do Moe and Joe shows, I always ask for big money if we do them together. But Joe and I had a great run, and it was fun.

Now that I've told my side of the Moe and Joe story, I thought it was only fair that I gave Joe his chance to tell his version:

♫

"At the time that I came up with the Moe and Joe idea, I had a string of solo hits going. And Moe had a string of hits going. That's what made our Moe and Joe stage show so exciting. He would sing all of his hits, and then I'd sing mine, and then we'd team up together for all of our duet hits. It was (and still is) a concert that very few country acts could match.

Our Moe and Joe songs really touched people. Many folks could relate to the silly things that went on in those songs. They could relate to all the trouble me and Moe found ourselves in. But I never dreamed that we would come up with as many great songs as we did.

The secret to Moe and Joe was the feel-good songs that we did. They just made the audience feel good, or smile or laugh when they heard them. Moe and Joe didn't do any serious or sad ballads. Individually, Moe and I both did many, many sad ballads. But as a duo, we did just the opposite.

When Moe and Joe was the hottest act in country music, Moe's band called it "MoeJoe Mania." And it was! We would sign autographs for more than two hours each night after our concerts, and we still couldn't get to everyone. One of the autographs I remember the most was the time a woman asked us to sign her chest. She pulled down her top, and wanted Moe to sign one and me to sign the other. It got pretty crazy back then. But it was all in good fun.

One crazy night, Moe and I raced our tour buses. I had my own bus, and Moe had his own. We had our regular bus drivers sit in the back, and Moe drove his bus, and I drove mine. As we raced, we talked to each other over the CB radio. We didn't have cell phones back then, and the CB radio was the big thing. And we raced a long time, side by side, going down the interstate.

Moe has a very dry sense of humor. He can be so funny over the least little thing. He is very clever and very sharp. And he loves to work. He would still work 364 days a year if he could find a stage to get on. He loves to perform!

As he mentioned, he didn't like putting on the dress for the "Where's the Dress?" video! Moe told me, "Joe, I've got too many rodeo friends and too many cowboy friends. I can't wear a dress. There ain't no way I can dress up like that. I would never be able to live it down and I'd never hear the end of it from all my friends."

But when he saw me with all the women's makeup on, sitting there in that dress and even wearing high heel shoes, he laughed, "If you are man enough to do it, I will go ahead and do it too." It was a fun video to make.

We were onstage at Billy Bob's, getting ready to sing "Where's the Dress?." This was after the big lawsuit over the song, and I told the crowd, "That little pecker head Boy George sued us, didn't he Moe?"

Moe said, "Yes, he did. He sued us for a lot of money."

I asked him, "Moe, what will we do if we ever see that guy? If he ever comes to one of our shows or we happen to run into him, what do you think will happen?"

Moe stood there, and finally said, "I'll tell you what we're gonna do. We'll gather up and whip his ass!"

The Moe and Joe days were a hell of a ride. And we enjoyed the heck out of it. There were a lot of parties. There was a lot of drinking. Moe did most of that. We did a tour of the west coast, and a lot of crazy things happened. Most of those things, I would be afraid to tell, but it was fun just to wake up and know that we were going to get to do another show later that night.

There is one word that sums up our Moe and Joe show, especially today: it's "magic." Something happens when we get onstage together. It's magical. We really play off of each other onstage. And the audience really gets into it.

When I think back on the heyday of Moe and Joe, I can describe it like this… it was big. It was fun. It was exciting. But there was a lot of work to it too. We worked at finding great songs. And we traveled so much.

And today, we still do a few shows together each year. And each one is magical. It is still so much fun when we can get onstage together. We are brothers from different mothers. I kind of feel that way. I know that I can pick up the phone and call Moe anytime. And he knows he can always call me and I'll be there."

– Joe Stampley

♫

Many years after all of our Moe and Joe hits, Tim McGraw and Kenny Chesney were doing a tour together, and they liked to end their concert every night with the Moe and Joe song "Good Ol' Boys."

On their last tour date, their management called me and Joe, and asked if we would be their surprise guests. When they started singing the song, Joe and I walked out onstage. And Tim and Kenny both bowed down to us and said, "We are not worthy!" It was a cool show.

THE LEGENDS

I've been very blessed with a great career. I thank God for the life and success I have had. I've recorded many more hit songs than I could ever do in one concert. When fans come up and say, "You are my favorite country singer", I sincerely respond with, "Thank you very much." But quite often, someone will tell me, "Moe, you are a legend."

To that, I have to say no, I do not agree. I will tell you about some legends. I not only got to work with them, but I also became great friends with them. These are the true legends.

♫

George Jones – When I was younger, I had a flat-top haircut just like George. I loved his songs. I still remember the first time I ever talked to him: I was on an all-night radio show with Billy Coe in Des Moines, Iowa. I had a few hit records by then, and we were doing the radio show on their 100,000 watt station. We were on the air, and they said that they had someone who wanted to talk to me. They put the caller on the air, and it was George Jones and Tammy Wynette! They said, "We just want to tell you that we love your music. You are real traditional country music, and we love you." Oh my God! It just thrilled me to death.

I ended up doing a lot of shows with George, and I got to know him very well. We used to play at his Possum Holler club in Nashville. That was one of the funnest places. Everyone would be there. I was just in awe of Jones.

George and I drank together, and we got pretty wild together. There is one story that I remember, very vaguely, because we were very intoxicated at the time. We flew from Dallas to Nashville. Me and George were in first class, and we had seats together. And we drank a ton of whiskey between Dallas and Nashville.

When we got to Nashville, George asked me, "Where are ya going?"

I said, "I have a session in a few hours."

"I'll take you," he said. He had a corvette, and we got in and he took off. He was going 90 miles an hour, and we were heading out of Nashville. I yelled, "Where are we going, George?"

He said, "We're headin' to Alabama!"

I yelled, "George, I've got to be at my session!" And I was finally able to talk him into turning around so I could get back. It was one wild night.

I was also one of the very first people to hear George Jones sing his all-time greatest song. I was staying at the Maxwell House Hotel. George had been down in the lounge. My booking agent was with him, and he told George that I was up in my room. I heard a knock on the door, and when I answered, there stood George with his guitar… and he was completely loaded. He was ready to fall down.

I told George to come in, as he slurred, "I want you to hear this song." George sat on my bed and started strumming his guitar. Then he sang, "He said I'll love you till I die…" He sang all of "He Stopped Loving Her Today."

I yelled, "George, where did you get that song?!"

He said, "I ain't gonna tell ya."

"Who wrote it?" I asked.

He answered, "I ain't telling you. But I will get it to you…" Then he continued, "I can't cut it. I'm all screwed up with the booze. I'll get it to your producer because this will be a big hit for you."

I was so excited! I knew it was a huge hit song. But of course, my producer never heard from George. And the next time I heard that song was when George was singing it on the radio. I still sing it in concert today. But no one could ever do it like George.

In 2009, Don Ayers with 'County Music People UK' asked George about me. I was so touched and humbled at George's response. His exact words were, "I have always loved Moe's music. He is what Country Music is all about. When Moe sings a song, it has been sung. I just love the guy and his work. We have been friends for many years."

♫

Tammy Wynette – I loved Tammy Wynette. She was just the sweetest lady. I was walking down 16th Avenue once, and it was snowing and cold in Nashville. As I walked, a Rolls-Royce pulled up next to me.

The back window came down, and there inside sat Tammy Wynette. She leaned out the window and yelled, "I love you Moe Bandy!"

I smiled and said, "I love you too Tammy." She drove away, and those were the last words I ever said to Tammy.

♫

Merle Haggard – Merle Haggard was the all-around country star. He could do it all. I loved Merle. He wrote so good. He was a good musician, and a great, great singer and entertainer.

I worked quite a few shows with Merle. He had a club on Lake Shasta, where he had his boat. And to get to the club, we had to drive our bus up the side of a mountain that had no guardrails. You looked straight down over the cliff. The front of the bus would be hanging over the edge as we made each turn. That was the scariest bus ride that I've ever been on. A couple of my guys wouldn't come back down the mountain on the bus. They got rides in cars.

We played the club, and then I stayed a couple days on a boat that was docked next to Merle's. I brought my kids there with me. One day, I went onto Merle's boat and he had a big hole right in the middle of the floor. He was holding a fishing pole with the line down that hole. And he was watching TV and fishing at same time!

The Hag was the ultimate. I also got to see him write a song. We were in London England; Leona Williams was there, and Bonnie Owens was also there. They invited me to Merle's room, and when I walked in, they were writing a song, called "Let's Sing a Family Song." I ended up singing harmony with them as they wrote. And as I watched him write down the words on the paper as they came to him, I thought, "What a thrill to be able to see the master in action."

I once asked Merle, "How can I get one of those good songs of yours?" And he pitched me a song called, "Don't Sing Me No Songs About Texas." It was a real hot swing song. And Merle came in and sang it with me. You can find it on my album, "Devoted To Your Memory."

♫

Conway Twitty – I did quite a few shows with Conway Twitty. We worked a lot of TV shows and several concerts together. I really respected Conway. He was always such a professional. He also did me a special favor. One of my wife's cousins was a huge Conway fan; she was one of those who just went crazy for him. And when Conway played a rodeo in San Antonio, he let me bring my wife and her cousin onto his bus to meet him. He took the time to visit with them. He really went out of his way to be nice to everyone. I always thought a lot of Conway.

♫

Johnny Cash – I will never forget New Year's Eve 1981. I went to celebrate at Billy Bob's in Fort Worth, Texas. I didn't perform, I just went as a guest. I thought it would be a good place to ring in 1982. Boy, was it. You could say they had a pretty good lineup on stage that night. Comedy legend Bob Hope was there, along with Johnny Cash and his wife June Carter Cash. And Chuck Berry also performed! Razzy Bailey was also on the bill. And at the end of the night, we all sang "Auld Lang Syne." It was a great way to start the New Year.

♫

Minnie Pearl – We were doing the TV show "Nashville Now" with Ralph Emery. And the show had their own music equipment and drums, but my drummer, Nick Ochoa, needed his drum sticks, so he went back to get them from our bus.

All of our gear was stored in a compartment under the bus, and his sticks were underneath everything. So he had to pull out all of the equipment and instruments, and he was standing there on the sidewalk, trying to get it all out. Right then, Minnie Pearl walked by. She was in her costume, with her hat with the price tag and everything. She looked at Nick unloading the bus all by himself and laughed, "So you want to be in show business, huh?"

♫

Marty Robbins – Marty Robbins was one of my heroes. I loved Marty. He was so good. He was such a great showman. We worked together over in Europe, and we did several tours over there. We did the Wembley Festival, and we also played in Germany and Sweden. We did some really big package shows with Marty, me, Jerry Lee Lewis, Tammy Wynette, Freddy Fender, and Conway Twitty. We were in Holland, and Freddy Fender was singing some of his Mexican songs. And Marty could sing every one of them with him.

Later, when Joe Stampley and I were hot and had won all of our awards, we were on a show with Marty, and the promoter told us that Marty was going to open for me and Joe. I said, "Oh no. That is terrible.

He shouldn't go on before us," but the promoter insisted, saying, "That's the way I want it. You guys are hot." I didn't think it was right, and I didn't want to do it. Yes, we were hot right then, but Marty Robbins was a legend.

And Marty did not take it well. When the promoter told him the schedule, Marty did not like it at all. And when he went out to do his forty-five minutes, he refused to end his show. He just kept singing. He ended up doing three hours! They couldn't pull him off the stage with a bulldozer. He did every song he ever knew, and a few that he didn't. By the time me and Joe got out there, the crowd was worn out and leaving.

I think this would be a good place to give a little advice to some of the new, "hot" country acts. My advice is pretty simple… always be sure to be nice to your opening act. Let me tell you about a couple of artists who opened my shows. Thankfully, I was always nice to them!

I was in Hawaii, doing a tour of little clubs and bases there. I had several hits at the time. And this man kept telling me that there was a guy in the Navy who I really had to go hear sing. I kept putting them off, because I was tired from doing all of my own shows, and I didn't feel like going to see someone else.

But I finally went to this military club to see the guy. I walked in and saw this young man wearing a cowboy hat. And as soon as he stepped up to the microphone, I knew that he was great. He blew me away. Afterward, when they introduced me to him, he said, "Hi, I'm George Strait. And I am so thrilled to meet you Moe." He was really excited to meet me, and he got even more excited when I told him that I thought he was going to be a big star.

A few years later, George cut his first songs in Nashville and started opening my concerts for me. He opened for me on quite a few shows, then did two weeks at the Frontier Hotel in Las Vegas. It was me and George. For two weeks, we did our show every night and every day we would play golf. We played golf at the Vegas Country Club every single day.

I got to know George very well, and we got to be very close friends. He lived in San Antonio, and I did too. He lived out at the Dominion Golf Course, so we played golf out there quite a bit. We had a show in Springfield, Missouri one time. And we played golf, from the early morning right up to show time.

I had the honor of being there on the exact day that George Strait became a star. I was onstage when he moved from the opening act to the headliner. Yep, I was there... because that was the day that I went from being the headliner to being the opening act!

We were in Kansas City, and were going to play two shows that day. The promoter asked that George open the first show of the day, and then we switch and I open the second show. And that was the day that George passed me. From then on, when we did concerts together, I was the opening act and he closed the show. Of course, a few years later, he got so big that he didn't need any opening act at all!

It was just amazing, watching George's career take off. It was unbelievable. It was all George's talent. He was just one of those great singers, who don't come around very often. A few years ago, I went to see George in Las Vegas; he was playing at The Nugget, and we sat backstage visiting for a long time. I really admire what he's done in his life, on and off stage.

I also had another opening act that you might have heard of: his name was Garth Brooks. Garth opened my shows in Oklahoma several times. We played some of the big clubs there. And he has been such a good friend over the years. Garth has never forgotten me or any of the older acts.

When my daughter was a teenager, she loved Garth Brooks. And all of her friends loved him. They still do. When he came to do a concert in San Antonio, we got tickets for everyone, and I took my daughter and her friends. And when Garth saw me there, he brought us all onto his bus. He gave each person in my large group every T-shirt, every cap, every CD and photo that he had. He was so nice.

A few months later, Garth was playing at a big rodeo in Texas. My daughter went to the concert, and as she was walking down the aisle, one of Garth's band members yelled at her, "Hey, aren't you Moe Bandy's daughter?"

She said "Yes."

And they said, "Garth would want to see you." So they took her and her friends backstage to visit with him. That was very impressive to me.

When he played in Las Vegas a few years ago, I went to see him. I took six other people with me, including my wife Tami and my son. We went to Garth's show, and after it was over, he brought us all backstage, and he sat and talked to us for an hour.

I told Garth that if I was ever going to write a book on how to be a star, that I was going to put his picture on the cover. He handles his stardom so well. He really does. I am amazed at how he treats his fans, and how he treats the older singers. That really means a lot to me.

And I had one more opening act that would quickly turn into one of the biggest headliners in country music... we played Disneyland in February of 1981. And our opening act was a new group that was trying to get going. They loaded their stuff, all the instruments and gear, and went out and did their show. Then they tore it all down and started packing up as my band was getting ready to go on next. And that group was... Alabama. But that was probably one of the last times they had to work as their own roadies, because Alabama went on to have three #1 songs in 1981! They never opened for me again.

HEROES AND FRIENDS

I have so many Country Music heroes and friends. I'd have to do another book just to list all of those folks. But I am thankful for each one of them. Here's some memories of a few…

Gene Watson and I have been friends for many years. He's from Houston. I actually met him in the early 70s. We played a benefit together, and then started running into each other around Texas. I was celebrating my first big hit of "I Just Started Hatin' Cheatin' Songs Today."

But Gene was still trying to find his first hit. And he was getting very discouraged. Backstage before a show, he told me, "Moe, I am about ready to give it up. I'm frustrated. I'm trying to get a hit, and I'm doin' everything I can, but nothing is happening for me."

I told him, "When I got to that point, that's when everything finally happened for me." One year later, I hear him singing "Love in the Hot Afternoon" on the radio!

Gene and I got booked to play a concert in Nova Scotia, and when we got there, we found out we were playing in a hockey rink. It was a hockey rink, but the entire show was rinky dink! I can't tell you how screwed up the whole deal was, but I will try.

Just before we left for the show, the promoter called and said they didn't have a PA system. No sound system, speakers or anything! I thought, "What kind of gig is this?"

So I went to Nashville and bought a sound system. While I was in Nashville, I also hired a steel guitar player. I wanted to make sure we did this "big show" up right! We flew to New York to meet two other band members. But when we arrived, we found that the Canadian air strike had grounded all commercial flights, and that we would be stuck in New York until I could find a charter plane.

So I paid for a couple hotel rooms, and me and the band started lugging the entire PA system up to our room… on the 27th floor! While I searched for a plane, the show promoter called again. He said they didn't have any other star on the bill. And he wanted more than just me and Gene. Then he asked if one of my band members could sing. When I said, "Yes," he yelled, "Great! I will put them on the show bill and poster!" I told my bass player Bill Bowers, "Bill, today is the day you become a star!"

I finally found a plane that we could charter. It was a big DC-3, that had belonged to the Kennedys. We even had our own stewardess on the plane. I have no idea how much I had to pay for that flight from New York to Nova Scotia, but it was a lot.

As soon as the concert started, the MC introduced the "famous" Bill Bowers, all the way from Nashville, Tennessee! Bill had bought himself a fancy new shirt since he was now a "star." He sang a couple songs, and then Gene went on, and then I closed the show. And that was one of the first concerts Gene and I ever did together.

I always love to pick on Gene Watson. He is sometimes in a foul mood, and I love to pick on him, because I know I can always get a response. One night, he was playing a concert in Florida, and I happened to be nearby. I was off that night, so I went to the show. He didn't know I was in the audience. For some reason, Gene was wearing a cowboy hat. And it was the worst damn hat I have ever seen in my life. In the middle of his show, I walked right up to the stage and yelled, "Where did you get that taco you're wearing on your head?!" Gene just stood there speechless. I yelled, "That is the ugliest damn hat I've ever seen!"

We were doing a 'Country's Family Reunion' taping, and Gene and I sat next to each other. During that show, you are supposed to just jump in and add any comment or story that you have. It's all ad-libbed. But instead of him saying the stuff himself, Gene kept leaning over to me and whispering, "Tell them this…" and "Tell them that story."

I finally said, "What the hell do you think I am, a ventriloquist?!" I got a laugh when I said, "GENE wants to know…"

During that same TV taping, Gene finally started talking about his new CD. And he bragged about all the duets he had done with everybody who is anybody in country music… everybody but me! I told him, "I didn't get a call to be on your CD. I was sitting at home, warming up my voice. I kept waiting for the phone to ring."

He looked at me and said, "I lost your number." I still have people asking me, "Did Gene ever get your phone number?"

I like to go on the country music cruises with Gene. You can usually find him in the ship's casino. He loves to play the slots. And I like to have fun with him. I'll be walking out of the casino, and he'll stay in there gambling. But if I see some fans walking in, I'll point out where Gene is so that they can easily find him. After a couple of minutes, he'll have a big line of people wanting to meet him as he tries to play the slot machines! He is real serious when he's at the slots, and I like to mess that up anytime I can!

In 2016-17, Gene and I filmed the "Moe and Gene Show" for RFD TV. We got to sing a lot of songs. It showed us both in concert. We also filmed on location, as Gene took me to some classic car places, and as I took him to a bull ride. For a guy who's from Texas, Gene doesn't know a whole lot about cowboys. And when I tried to teach him how to feed a calf with a bottle, it made for pretty good TV.

When I asked Gene if he wanted to say anything in the book I was writing, he said, "I didn't know you could read a book, let alone write one!" After I hit him a couple times, he came up with some nicer stuff.

♫

"*Moe had his first two hits in 1974. And I got my first recording contract a year later. So our careers really took off at about the same time. When we were starting out, we both used to work in San Antonio Texas. He was playing at a a place called "The Golden Stallion" and I was working at "Bobby Barkers."*

Moe has changed so much from the way he was when I first met him. Back then he was a rowdy little sucker. The only thing he loved to do more than sing was fight. He was a bar room brawler. But he put all of that behind him and he is one of the nicest guys in the world.

Right from the start, we got to be very good friends. But we always liked to joke and poke fun at each other. And we just added to that each year and it became quite an act. If I was on stage and wore a vest or a cowboy hat, Moe would come up and make fun of me. He was always telling the crowd how I should never wear a cowboy hat since I wasn't a real cowboy.

Many times, he actually bought a ticket to my show just so he could come in and give me a hard time. I would be working on stage, doing my show, and Moe would walk right up to the front of the stage and start running his mouth at me. I was doing a live "Larry's Country Diner" show in Branson. And I had no idea he was even in town. So during my show, I was telling the crowd all the things I didn't like about Moe. And the whole time, they were hiding him back behind the counter on stage. And when he walked out to me, the whole crowd just went crazy.

Now it is kind of a given that we will kind of play off of each other. If I go on before him, I will slam him all I can. Because I know that he will get me back when he comes out. But it's all in fun. And we really are the best of friends. I love working with him. He is a great artist.

When I look back at of our careers, there are a couple of things that I credit for us both still being here, and still having great success today. We both sang traditional country. And we both stayed true to that. Moe's always leaned a little more toward the western and rodeo side, and mine didn't. But we both never left our traditional country sound. Our fans always knew what they would get when they came to see one of our shows. And if you buy a Gene Watson or Moe Bandy CD, you know what you'll hear. And that's real country music.

There is another thing we've both done over the years that really helped us keep all of the fans we made. And that is we both sign autographs and meet our fans after each show. We have done that for more than forty years. We always take time to shake hands and thank our fans for being there. So many of today's artists go out there and do a show, and then the minute they get through, they run off the stage and lock themselves on their bus. They don't sign autographs or meet their fans. And I'm pretty sure that forty years from now, those artists will be saying, "Boy, I wish someone wanted to meet me now."

Moe Bandy is one of the true great country music artists. And he has been true to the business. When he is on that stage, he gives it everything he's got. I really admire him for that. As a friend, I admire him even more. He is the real deal. I love him to death."

– Gene Watson

♫

Gene Watson is one of the greatest singers ever. He is just one of the all-time greatest in the history of country music. And people have finally realized how great his music is.

Imagine if Gene Watson would have quit the business before his first hit finally came. And of course, I was a "twelve-year overnight sensation"! It took me twelve years to finally have any kind of success on the charts. So here's a little advice for any person who might have a similar dream:

Persistence is the key. Stay with it. People get discouraged, and they want to quit and do something else. But you can't give up! You have to hang in there. I know a lot of people who were ready to quit. But all of a sudden, something happened and they hit. So stay with it.

♫

Johnny Russell and I played a show in Wichita, Kansas. Before the concert, we were having lunch on the very top floor of a big high-rise Holiday Inn. We looked out the window, and there were tornadoes dropping down everywhere. There were four or five tornadoes that we could see just from our window! Most of them were out in the country, but we could still see them since we were up so high. We watched them awhile as we ate our meal, and Johnny asked, "Do you think we ought to go somewhere else where it's safer?"

I said, "Yeah, I think that would be a good idea."

Then Johnny looked at his plate and said, "Maybe we could finish our food here first."

I have another Johnny Russell memory: we were in London, doing the Mervyn Conn Festival; and they brought me in, along with Conway and Loretta, Glen Campbell, Boxcar Willie and Johnny Russell. We happened to have a free night, so I booked us to play at this little club in London. But just before the show, I got laryngitis and I couldn't sing. So I asked Johnny Russell to fill in for me.

After his sound check, Johnny asked the club owner if there was a place to get something to eat. He wanted some American food. The owner said, "There's a Kentucky Fried Chicken just around the corner."

Johnny licked his lips and said, "Good! Go over there and get an 18-piece bucket of chicken." All my band members heard him, and they were thinking they were going to have some good chicken before the show. But they watched as Johnny ate every piece of that 18-piece bucket!

I'd like to add that Johnny Russell was also an amazing songwriter and singer. And he was one of the greatest showmen there ever was.

♫

There is one concert that I will never forget. It was in Denver, Colorado. I opened the show, then Hank Williams, Jr. followed me… and the main headliner was Jerry Lee Lewis. I had always loved Jerry Lee. He was just an amazing entertainer.

Before the show, I was backstage with Hank and Jerry Lee. And we had a fifth of whiskey sitting on the table. I didn't want to drink much, because I was getting ready to go on, but Jerry Lee was drinking that whiskey like it was iced tea! He drank almost the entire bottle.

When Jerry Lee walked out onstage, he asked the audience, "How'd you like Hank Williams, Jr?!" The crowd erupted with huge applause. Then he asked them, "How'd you like Moe Bandy?" And the crowd gave me a quieter round of pleasant applause. And Jerry Lee yelled, "Well, if you don't like Moe Bandy, you can kiss my ass!"

♫

Dottie West loved the way I said the word "woman." If you listen to one of my early hits, "It Was Always So Easy to Find an Unhappy Woman", I say the word "woman" as "wo-man." Dottie and I performed together at the Frontier Hotel in Las Vegas. We did a two week run there, and each night, she would bring me out during her part of the show and she'd tell me, "Say wo-man!" I just loved Dottie. She was such a sweet lady. I really enjoyed working with that wo-man.

♫

The Gatlins, Larry, Steve and Rudy, are some of my dearest and best friends. Larry Gatlin was one of the stars on the bill at the big Mervyn Conn Festival. That festival always booked so many country music stars each year. They would fly us all there on the same jet plane. If that plane would have crashed, country music would have come to an end. Everybody in country music was on it.

I played the festival, along with Larry Gatlin and the Gatlin Brothers. Phil Everly of the Everly Brothers was also on the show, and after our concert, a bunch of us were all sitting in the hotel lobby. Larry Gatlin came in after he had been partying a little bit... maybe quite a bit. We were passing a guitar around, and taking turns playing and singing there in the lobby. Larry sat down and sang a couple songs, and at the end of the second one, he flipped that guitar up in the air. He was going to catch it, but when it came down, it landed right on the top of his nose. Blood just went everywhere! It started pouring out of his nose and we had to take him to the hospital to get stitches. I still rib him about that. I say, "Yeah, that was a fancy little move you did with that guitar flip. Could you teach me how to do that?" He never laughs!

♫

I was booked to do a concert in West Palm Beach, Florida. The Britt family put on the show. They were very well-to-do. They were with the Goodyear rubber company. I eventually became very close friends with their entire family; I would stay with them when I came to Florida. They also had a big limo that they would let me use when I had a show anywhere in the state.

The Britt family were dear friends, and when they booked me to headline the show, they told me they wanted another singer to open for me. They were backing this young man, and the main reason for the show was to be able to put their singer in front of a big crowd.

So who was the guy who opened for me? It was John Anderson. Many years later, John would have huge hits including "Swingin'", "Straight Tequila Night", and "Black Sheep."

John was from Florida. He was very nervous that night, especially playing the big auditorium we were in. I thought he did OK, but at the time, he didn't sing like he does now. He hadn't found his own style yet. And to be honest, I didn't see his real talent back then. But once he'd found his own style, he just knocked everybody out. He has really become one of the great singers in country music.

In the spring of 2017, I was visiting with John. We both got to talking about our grandchildren, and John said, "Oh my gosh. They are the greatest thing in my life. When I come home from a tour, I pull in the driveway and see all of those little happy feet out there waiting for me!"

♫

When I think of my very closest friends in country music, I think of Gene Watson, and I also think of T.G. Sheppard. I am very close with T.G. He took me to Memphis this past year. He was going to kick off the Christmas celebration at Graceland, so he took me and Gus Arrendale with him. And when you go to Graceland with T.G., you go in style. He was friends with Elvis, and everyone at Graceland knows T.G. We got to see all the behind-the-scenes stuff there.

Johnny Lee is another very close friend. One reason that Johnny, T.G. and Gene are all great friends is we have all lasted so long. We have all survived. We've done enough concerts together and know each other so well, that we are true friends. I would do anything for those guys. They are my best friends. Of course, Johnny Lee is never at a loss for words. And he said he had a few to say here.

♫

"My autobiography "Still Lookin' for Love" came out a year ago (I had to get that plug in, Moe!). I was honored when Moe agreed to write the foreword for my book. And he said that my book is what led him to start thinking about writing his own.

Many years ago, when I found out I had colon cancer, Moe was one of the first people I told. We were playing golf in Branson. A few minutes after I broke the news to him. I was standing off to the side of him, about twenty yards away as he teed off. And his drive hit me right in the middle of my back! That ball hit me between my shoulder blades and knocked me down!

Moe felt so bad about it. When he ran over to help me up, I said, "I just told you I have cancer and you try to kill me with a golf ball?!"

When I had my cancer surgery, Moe was there when I came out of the operating room. When my anesthesia was wearing off, I opened my eyes, and Moe was standing over me. He said, "Johnny, this is what they took out of you during the surgery." He gave me a little Tupperware container. I opened it, and inside was a golf ball that he had covered in ketchup!

I still have that ball, still in the Tupperware today. Moe is one of my very best friends. We are there for each other. I would do anything for him."

– Johnny Lee

♫

Mickey Gilley was one of the kings of Branson during Branson's boom. His shows were always sold out. Not only did he sing his long list of #1s, but he had also found a comedian named Joey Riley; and when they started doing their show together, they drew people by the tens of thousands, year after year.

Mickey and I did a lot of concerts together. I also performed a year at his theater in Branson. He loved to play golf, and we played a lot of golf together over the years.

Today, Mickey is a walking miracle. He survived brain surgery, open heart surgery, and a horrible accident that paralyzed him for quite a while. It is a miracle that he is still here and still performing. And he is still a fantastic entertainer. We have always been good friends. I think the world of him.

♫

In 1983, I had a top ten duet with Becky Hobbs. Becky was a whole lot prettier than Joe Stampley, and she was just a little fireball. She had the hit "Jones on the Jukebox", and also wrote "Angels Among Us" for Alabama. Becky and I had a big hit with "Let's Get Over Them Together." She has a great story about the way we first met. It has to do with her grandma and donuts. I'll let her tell it.

♫

"The man who booked the Coffeeville Fair and Rodeo used to come in Goldie's Donuts in Coffeeville, Kansas. The shop was owned by my aunt and uncle, and my grandma Hobbs waited tables there. She served coffee and donuts, and flirted with the old guys who would come in each morning.

Lucky Me by Moe Bandy

One morning, the man who booked the acts for the fair stopped in, and Grandma asked him, "Who do you have playing the fair and rodeo this year?"

He said, "We've got Moe Bandy. But we're looking for a girl singer to open the show."

And Grandma said, "Well, my granddaughter sings!" And by the time their conversation had ended, grandma had talked him into booking me to open for Moe!

During the concert, I did my high-energy show and gave them everything I had. And it went really great. Afterward, I went to say hi to Moe. When I walked on his bus, he said, "My God, if you had a hit record, you would be dangerous!" Then he shocked me by asking, "Do you want to record a duet?"

I shouted, "I sure would!"

A short time later, Moe called and told me he had a song for us to do. When we went into the studio to record "Let's Get Over Them Together", we were supposed to cut it in the key of D. But Ray Baker bumped it up to E Flat, and he didn't tell me or Moe. As we were singing, I kept thinking, "God that feels high." It was really at the top of my range when I got to the high part, but I survived it, and we laid the song down. But when we perform it live today, we usually do it in D.

I didn't have a record deal when I cut the duet with Moe. Heck, my grandma at the donut shop was my manager! But when my song with Moe went to the top ten, Len Shultz signed me to a record deal with Capital EMI, just on the strength of that one song.

Whenever we work together, it is so much fun. We have a great friendship. We genuinely like each other, and I think the audience can see that. Moe was always real nice. He still has a number of the same band members that he had back in the 80s. That is really the sign of a good person. If you can keep your musicians over all those years, you must be a pretty great guy.

The cool thing about Moe and me is that even though we don't get to sing together all that much, when we do have the chance, it's like no time has passed. And for some reason, our voices go well together.

Everybody can relate to Moe. Guys like him because they know he's a good ol' boy. And women like him because he's cute and funny. He also has a kind of vulnerability about himself. To me, Moe is kind of the boy next door. That might sound funny since he is over 70 years old. But he still has an innocence and a sweetness about him."

– Becky Hobbs

♫

Becky Hobbs is a great entertainer. After "Let's Get Over Them Together", we recorded another duet. It didn't turn out to be a big hit, but it was a nice little song called, "Pardon Me." Becky and I were doing a concert together right after "Pardon Me" was released, but I didn't know the words to the song, so we wrote the lyrics on a piece of paper and we taped it to Becky's back! When it came my turn to sing, she would turn her back to me and I'd read the words. We started off trying to hide it, but we finally showed the audience what we were doing, and they thought it was funny. Becky said, "Moe, you took the words right off my back!"

♫

One my dearest friends is Jimmy Capps. Jimmy plays the Sheriff on Larry's Country Diner. But he has also played on some of the biggest hits that were ever made in Nashville. He played on everything from "He Stopped Loving Her Today" for George Jones, to "Stand By Your Man" for Tammy Wynette, to "Elvira" for The Oak Ridge Boys. Jimmy also played on almost all of my hits. I asked Jimmy if he remembered how we first met.

♫

"I was part of a booking agency in the late 60s and early 70s. And we booked Moe for a show. He sang standards and songs that were hits for other people, because he didn't have any hits of his own. I met Moe for the first time that night.

From the very first time I saw him, I just knew that Moe had something. He had a certain kind of magnetism. He could relate to the people, and they could relate to him.

A short time later, I was booked to play on one of Moe's recording sessions; and that was the first of many, many sessions that I would play with him. I played on "Hank Williams, You Wrote My Life." I played electric guitar on that song.

Ray Baker was a great producer for Moe. Ray knew the songs that would fit his voice. Back when Moe was recording all of those hits, just one after another, that was back when you had to really sing in the studio. If you missed a note, you had to go back and do it over until you got it right. You had to really have talent back then. And he had it.

When he plays on the Opry today, the audience just loves him. They just go crazy over his songs. And when he walks out on that stage, he takes over. You know who the lead horse is. And he is such a professional onstage. I think he learned a lot of that from doing two shows a day at his theater in Branson.

A funny thing happened at one of our "Country's Family Reunion" tapings. My wife Michele had bought me a new Cinch western shirt. It was purple, with a very unique design. I walked in, and the first person I saw was Moe, and he was wearing the exact same shirt! And neither of us had another one to change into. But Moe found a black vest, and he put that on over his shirt to make us look a little different. But if you watch that show, you can still see that we have on identical shirts.

A few years ago, Moe came to me and said, "I would like you to produce an album on me." I said, "I would be honored." So we started looking for material. But it took us a couple years to complete the album. Since he lives in Branson, and I live in Nashville, it took us a long time. But it was worth all of the time and effort. His "Lucky Me" album is really special. I am very proud of that album. Moe is singing better now than he has ever sung. And "Lucky Me" turned out so great that we are going to record a new album together.

If you ever meet Moe, you will love him. I guarantee you that you will love him. He treats everybody so good. He treats everyone with so much respect, and he appreciates his fans. He is also a very humble man. He is a gentle, humble man. And I am proud to call him my friend."

– Jimmy Capps, Grand Ole Opry Staff Band

♫

I would also like to say that I love all the guys who are legends on the Texas music scene. Darrell McCall and Tony Booth are so great. And Johnny Bush is one of my favorites, as well as one of my best friends. I have been doing a lot of shows with those guys over the last few years.

Johnny Bush had a great band called The Bandoleros. They did the shuffle type music. And I just idolized Johnny. They traveled in a camper, and I can still remember the day I walked onto Johnny's camper! I told him, "I'm going to Nashville and try to record." Then I asked him, "Do you know where I can get some songs?" He got me with a writer and I did a couple of his songs. And they played those on the radio a little in Texas. I will always be grateful for the help that Johnny gave me.

THE CHAMP

Have you ever wanted to go on a nice, peaceful European vacation? If so, never go with a country music artist!

We were booked for a 30-day tour all over Europe. Three weeks into the tour, we had our first night off. And our group was booked to stay in a huge, old castle. We had an English band that was traveling with us, and we were all so crazy back then, that poor English group didn't know what to think. We had them so screwed up. By the time we left, they were doing all kinds of stupid stuff.

Since this was our first night off in three weeks, we decided that we were really going to party… a lot more than our usual partying! We all got so drunk and started running all around that old castle like idiots. Then we ran outside. It was a foggy night like you see in the old horror movies. And right next to the castle, they had a graveyard. And for some reason, there was an empty casket sitting at the entrance to the cemetery!

At the time, I had two twin brothers who worked for me. Greg Faile played lead guitar for me for twelve years, and his twin brother Gary played drums. Greg would do anything. If you bet him money, and dared him to do something, he would do it. And usually the person who dared him to do something was his twin brother.

Well, someone bet Greg that he wouldn't get in that casket in the cemetery! He said, "I'll do it for a hundred dollars." In an instant, we had taken up a collection. Greg walked up to the casket, and slowly got inside and laid down. As soon as he did, we ran over and slammed the lid down. We started putting rocks and dirt on top of it. Greg couldn't get out. He was screamin' and hollerin', and we finally let him out.

The next day, we visited the Loch Ness Lake, where the famous Loch Ness monster is supposed to be hiding. We enjoyed the lake, but we never spotted the monster. But a funny thing happened when we got back from the lake…

We went to a bar, and there was a huge ashtray sitting on a table. There was all kinds of stuff in it. It was filled with cigarette butts, and even an old sandwich that was covered in ashes. Someone said to Greg Faile, "I betcha won't eat that." Greg looked at it and said, "For enough money, I will." We took up another collection and said, "We'll give you a hundred dollars if you eat everything that's in that ashtray." And guess what… he ate the entire thing! The cigarette butts and everything. The bartender yelled, "Oh, you bloody Americans!"

When you are on the road, you never know what is going to happen. Here are just a few stories for you.

We were getting ready for a show in Oklahoma. We were in the parking lot, when a man came running up to the bus. The guy was on drugs or something, but we didn't know it at the time.

When Richard, my road manager, opened the bus door, this guy jumped inside and pulled out a knife. He pointed it an inch away from Richard's throat. I was in the front seat, and when I saw what was happening, I jumped up and hit that guy as hard as I could.

And I hit him just perfect. He flew up and hit the windshield, and was totally knocked out. He fell down the bus stairs and landed outside the bus. Richard and I looked at each other, and then Richard got behind the steering wheel and drove off. We left the man lying there on the asphalt.

We made a short drive to our hotel and when we got there, I called the police. I told them that the man had pulled a knife on us and I had hit him and knocked him out. By the time I called them, the police had already found the guy and they asked me, "Moe, what in the world did you hit him with? We could barely get him to wake up."

♫

We played at a big coliseum in El Paso. After I'd signed autographs for everyone, the manager of the place came up and started giving us hell about paying him a commission. He wanted a big cut of everything that we'd sold at the merchandise table. He wasn't very professional about it all, and he started cussing me in Spanish. And he didn't have a clue that I know a lot of Spanish. I could tell that he was cursing me.

He started following me, and then he pushed me in the back. Wrong thing to do! I turned around and just laid him out with one punch. I told my band, "Pack up!" We quickly loaded the bus as Bruce, our driver, was getting changed. I yelled, "Bruce, get behind the wheel and let's go!

You can change clothes later." We were gone before the manager woke up. But for a while, I had a warrant out for me in El Paso because of that incident.

♫

I was at the Peddlers Inn in Nashville. It happened to be my birthday, but I wasn't in a celebrating mood. I was sitting with the man who wrote "Hank Williams, You Wrote My Life." Ray Baker was also with us. We were sitting at a table, when a great big guy came up to me, and said, "I pitched you a song and you didn't cut it. I ought to whip your ass."

I tried to laugh him off, but he kept on, saying: "I pitched it to ya and it's a good song. You should cut it."

I wasn't in a good mood to begin with. And this guy just kept on yelling about me not recording his song. Finally, I'd had enough, and I said, "Ya know the reason I didn't cut your song is because it was a piece of shit."

He walked off, but then he turned around and came back. Again, he said, "I still think you ought to cut my song." I stood up and hit him all the way across the room. I jumped on him and just beat the crap out of him. When I finally stopped, they had to carry him out. But as they were carrying him, he yelled, "Cheap shot!" With that, I hit him harder than I have ever hit anyone. The punch not only knocked him down, but all the guys who were carrying him also fell down!

The next day, I got a call from Stan Berg. Stan was the head of Warner Brothers. He said, "Moe, I am going to mow your lawn. I'm gonna carry your luggage, anything you want!" Then he told me that the same guy had hit him and broken his nose, and he'd had to have surgery. The next day, I recorded the song "The Champ."

♫

Richard Hill and I needed a ride to our hotel at the Hall of Fame Motor Inn. And we got a ride from another guy. The guy was a bass player, but we didn't know him very well.

I was in the front seat with the guy, and we had a few words and got into a fight. As we pulled into the hotel parking lot, the guy pulled out a gun and put it right next to my head. Richard was in the backseat, and I could tell that he was petrified as he looked at the gun touching my face.

I angrily said, "Look at this Richard! This stupid son of a bitch thinks he's going to shoot me." I turned to the guy and said, "You stupid piece of shit."

Richard started pleading with me, "Moe, please be quiet!" but I kept on, saying, "Look at this nitwit. He's playing cops and robbers. He can stick that gun up his ass." And I just opened the car door and walked into the hotel. I never looked back. But I could hear Richard running right behind me the whole way.

♫

Please don't let these stories fool you. I'm not trying to sound like I'm a tough guy. I am not a tough guy. And I got my butt kicked many times. I got into a lot of fights, mostly when I had been drinking. But I would never take any crap from anyone. I still won't.

COACH ROYAL

"As long as a person doesn't admit he is defeated, he is not defeated. He's just a little behind and isn't through fighting."

– Coach Darrell Royal

♫

Darrell Royal was one of the greatest college football coaches of all time. He served as head coach at the University of Texas at Austin from 1957 to 1976. Coach Royal was a Texas legend. But why would a football coach get his own chapter in the autobiography of a country music singer? The answer is easy: Coach Royal affected my life probably more than any other man. And he eventually saved my life.

My dad loved Texas University football. All of our family did, but my dad wouldn't miss a game. He was just a fanatic about it. And we loved the Texas coach Darrell Royal. Coach Royal was my hero. And I never dreamed that I would meet him.

After I had a couple hits songs, I played a show in San Antonio, and Coach Royal came to see me. I found out that Coach was a huge country music fan, and after the show, we visited a little and he told me that he lived in a place called Onion Creek. It was on the south side of Austin.

Coach Royal asked me, "Do you play golf?"

I answered, "No sir."

He said, "You are going to play. We're going to start playing golf together." So I went up to Onion Creek and we starting playing golf. And we quickly became very good friends.

Coach Royal's favorite thing in the world was to get some guitar players and singers together, and sit around in a circle and play. Willie Nelson was a good friend of Coach Royal, and Willie was at a lot of those guitar pulls. Coach Royal didn't play an instrument himself, but he loved listening to music at his pickin' parties. And he was very serious about these guitar pull sessions. We would have a bunch of people together in a room, and sometimes people would start talking and visiting, and Coach would jump up and yell, "Red light! If you can't be quiet, leave the room! We are going to listen to music!" When he yelled, "Red light!", that meant to shut up so he could hear the music.

Ernest Owen, one of our friends had a party bus. It had big couches all around the inside. And we drove it all over Dallas, as we played music and sang for Coach Royal all night. At another guitar pull, we had Willie Nelson, Tom T. Hall, Walt Garrison, the great Cowboy football player, and me. Willie played us songs he hadn't recorded yet that would go on to be big hits, and Coach Royal just sat there, eating it all up.

I was in Lubbock, Texas when Coach Royal called me and asked, "Are you coming to the game today? We're playing Texas Tech."

I said, "I'd love to, if you can get me a ticket."

Well, he did much more than that. He took me into the locker room just before the game, and he told me, "You have to see this guy. He is something else." It turned out to be Earl Campbell. Earl was lying on a table, and they were giving him a rub down. His legs were as big as tree trunks! Earl looked up at me and said, "Hey Moe Bandy." From then on, every time he saw me, Earl would never call me by just my first name. He always said, "Hi Moe Bandy. Good to see you Moe Bandy", or "Hey Moe Bandy, come over here."

Earl Campbell ran all over Texas Tech that day. He was so fast. And I had an up-close view, as I stood on the sidelines with the players! It was almost too close, when Earl almost ran over me on one play. After the game, he came up and smiled, "Moe Bandy, when you're on the sidelines, be sure to stand back a little bit, 'cause I'm comin' through!"

I spent many years watching Earl Campbell "comin' through", throughout most of his college and professional career. And when Earl went to play for the Houston Oilers, I was already close friends with his coach, Bum Phillips. Bum was a big fan of mine, and he invited me to a game. I was also asked to sing the National Anthem before the Oilers played on a Monday Night Football game.

When Houston played the Green Bay Packers, Coach Phillips asked me to fly on the team plane with them. I also brought along my guitar player Richard Hill. When we got to Green Bay, I rode on the bus with the team to the stadium. And as I walked into the locker room, I was surprised to see the star quarterback, Kenny Stabler, and some other players sitting with their helmets on, and they were each smoking a cigarette! The coach yelled, "Time to put your cigs out. We've got a game to play!"

Just before the game, Bum Phillips grabbed me and said, "We're flying back on the plane. You brought your guitar, didn't you?"

I said, "No, I didn't." So Bum told Richard Hill to go find a guitar and buy it. As the pre-game ceremony got underway, Richard took off in search of a guitar.

Did I mention that Richard liked to drink? Yeah, he did. He hailed a cab to go looking for a guitar shop, but first, he asked the driver to stop at a liquor store. Richard bought a big bottle of whiskey, and he sat in the back seat drinking, as the cab driver tried to find a guitar. They finally found one, Richard purchased it, and headed back to the game. But by the time they got back, he had finished off that entire bottle of booze.

When he came in, Richard was drunker than a skunk. The game was going on, and I looked up and saw Richard walking right down the sideline with that guitar in his hand! Coach Phillips also saw him coming down the line, and yelled, "We've found our guitar!"

When we flew back with the team, Earl Campbell got on the loud speaker and announced, "OK, let's all pay attention. We have Moe Bandy here, and he's going to sing us some songs. Let's all listen." I ended up singing all of my hits for the team. We sang all the way home.

Coach Phillips also invited me to go to Oakland with the team for a playoff game. I took Richard with me again. We got there the night before the game and went to a club called The Saddle Rack in San Jose. It was a big club that I had played at before, but we got so drunk that night. The club had a barber's chair that they laid you back in, and they would pour whiskey right down your throat. The next day, when we went to the game, Richard and I were both hungover so bad.

The Oilers also felt bad because lost their playoff game. And when we flew back on the team plane, everyone was down in the dumps. Finally, Coach Phillips told me, "Get your guitar and play us some music."

Kenny Stabler liked my music. And we became big buddies. We got to know each other pretty good, and when Joe Stampley and I opened the "Moe and Joe" club, he came out to party with us. We got him up onstage and he sang, "Good Ol' Boys" with us. They filmed that show and put a clip of it into a special NFL films documentary on Kenny Stabler.

♫

I was very close with Coach Phillips, but Coach Darrell Royal really became like a second father to me. Coach Royal was one of the most successful coaches in the history of college football, but he chose to retire when he was just fifty-two years old. I'm pretty sure that he quit just so that he could pursue his love of music. All he wanted to do was listen to country music and play golf.

After he retired, Coach Royal started hosting a golf tournament. I always played in it, and I got to meet and become friends with a lot of celebrities. One of those was baseball hall-of-famer Johnny Bench. We became good buddies, and played a lot of golf together. I have never seen a human being hit a golf ball so far in my life as Johnny did. He was a great golfer. He was also a big fan of country music. He even sang a little bit, and once appeared on an episode of "Hee Haw."

I also met the great actor James Garner through Coach Royal. James was known for his roles in "Maverick" and "The Rockford Files." James and Coach Royal were friends, and I got to spend a lot of time with him. He played in a lot of my golf tournaments. One year, I had a birthday while I was in Los Angeles, and James Garner had a birthday party for me at his house. He was a huge country music fan, and I loved him.

In 2011, I heard that Coach Royal had been diagnosed with Alzheimer's Disease. My wife and I made plans to go visit him. He and his wife, Edith, were living in a nursing home. It was like a nice apartment. I had called Coach and told him I was coming to see him, and when I got there, he was waiting out front for me. He also had some of his former players there to see him. Coach was losing his memory at the time, and it was frustrating for him.

I went back a short time later, and I took my granddaughter Brittney with me. She had graduated from Texas University, and she was in awe of Coach Royal. Richard Hill also came with us. Coach Royal loved Richard. But I was shocked to see how much Coach's Alzheimer's Disease had progressed since my last visit.

I brought my guitar along so that I could play some music for Coach. The nursing home workers also gathered some other residents together, so we had a little crowd watching as I sang. I wasn't sure if he remembered who I was, but Coach clapped and sang along. And then

1980's promo photo

With Merle Haggard at Billy Bob's, Fort Worth, Texas.
Courtesy Charles E. Wilkins

The photographer told me to look mean.

The photographer told me to try to look sexy.

Michael Martin Murphey, Ricky Skaggs and Sharon White

The Kings of Branson. Mickey Gilley, Roy Clark and Moe Bandy

They were beating down the door of my theater in
Branson.

Even Jed Clampett, Buddy Ebsen came to see my show
in Branson.

Filming the movie "Gordy." Me, Boxcar Willie, Roy Clark, Sybil Robson Orr and Tom Lester

Singing with my dad

With my mom

Visiting with my mom and dad

Moe, Loretta Lynn, Glen Campbell and Boxcar Willie, July 1992

Singing for President Bush in Branson. Glen Campbell, Jim Stafford, Boxcar Willie and Loretta Lynn also joined the President and First Lady.

To Lisa
with Warm Best Wishes — with great
pride in your Dad — Love — Gg Bush
Oct. 1989

President Bush signed this photo to my daughter in 1989

To Lisa Bandy —
From Camp David with Love
Gg Bush

At Camp David
with President
Bush and
my daughter
Lisa

Having a ball with
Crystal Gayle on the
Bush for President
campaign bus

To Moe ~ A White House "smash".
Thanks, my friend
Gg Bush

Singing for the President at the White House

Giving President Bush my Alvarez guitar

Singing for the President. President Bush is on the left.

How often do you get a hug like this from the President of the United States?

To Moe Bandy
with best wishes,

Gg Bush   Barbara Bush

With President Bush and my great friend,
Woody Bowles.

Country Music Month, 1990

By the President of the United States of America

A Proclamation

Whether they tap their feet to the spirited sound of bluegrass or quietly hum along with the soulful melodies of traditional ballads, millions of Americans—and, indeed, fans around the world—enjoy listening to country music each day. However, country music is more than a favorite source of entertainment; it is also a rich and colorful expression of the hopes, experiences, and values of the American people.

Encompassing a wide range of musical genres, from folk songs and religious hymns to rhythm and blues, country music reflects our Nation's cultural diversity as well as the aspirations and ideals that unite us. It springs from the heart of America and speaks eloquently of our history, our faith in God, our devotion to family, and our appreciation for the value of freedom and hard work. With its simple melodies and timeless, universal themes, country music appeals to listeners of all ages and from all walks of life.

The popularity of country music, both throughout the Nation and throughout the world, is a great tribute to generations of talented American composers, musicians, lyricists, and singers. This month, we gratefully acknowledge their many gifts to us and proudly celebrate the uniquely American art form that is country music.

The Congress, by House Joint Resolution 603, has designated October 1990 as "Country Music Month" and has authorized and requested the President to issue a proclamation in observance of this month.

NOW, THEREFORE, I, GEORGE BUSH, President of the United States of America, do hereby proclaim October 1990 as Country Music Month. I invite all Americans to observe this month with appropriate ceremonies and activities.

IN WITNESS WHEREOF, I have hereunto set my hand this twelfth day of October, in the year of our Lord nineteen hundred and ninety, and of the Independence of the United States of America the two hundred and fifteenth.

To Moe—
George Bush
My Friend. Good Luck
George Bush

President Bush autographed this official proclamation for me.

President Bush autographed this photo of the two of us.

Visiting with First Lady Barbara Bush.

GEORGE BUSH

August 14, 2008

Dear Moe,

On my return from China yesterday, your "Mama"
disc was on my desk. Barbara and I love those
songs. In fact, we put them on at bedtime; and
in joy and tranquility, I went sound asleep. I don't
think it was the jet lag; I think it was the wonders
of your music.

Warmest regards, old friend.

Sincerely,

[signature]

Signed letter from President George Bush, August 2008

Enjoying a visit to President Bush's home in Maine.

With President Bush and Mrs. Bush at their home in Kennebunkport Maine.

With my great friend Mike Hud Hudson and brother
Mike. Courtesy Charles E. Wilkins.

Sean Gleason, CEO of the PBR and Randy Bernard, former CEO

Visiting with my pal Cody Lambert

With rodeo great Larry Mahan

Singing with my buddy Justin McBride on the Opry

With Gene Watson and my pal Flint Rasmussen

My brother Mike, me, Sean Gleason and Gus Arrendale

Playing the Grand Ole Opry

I love Loretta Lynn

Accepting an award for my work for children's organ transplants.

Never a dull moment with Johnny Lee

Let the crowd in and let's do a show!

TG Sheppard,
Kelly Lang, Moe,
Tami Bandy,
Gus Arrendale,
Karen McEntire

With the great Garth Brooks

Moe and Tami. Our wedding photo, June 25, 2008.

Watch your back
around
T. Graham Brown

With Jean Shepard, March 2009

George Jones signed this photo of the two of
us on stage.

Having fun with Gary Morris at the Fan Fair IFCO
show.

With my wife Tami at the Ernest Tubb Record Shop in Nashville

Makaya

Kylar and Kaden

David Frizzell, Jimmy Fortune, Moe and Joe Stampley

Visiting with Daniel O'Donnell and Ray Stevens

Lorianne Crook feeds me cake as Charlie Chase watches

With Jennifer Herron, the host of the Ernest Tubb Midnite Jamboree

My #1 fan and dear friend Betty Urbanek. Betty took many of the photos in this book over the last 40 years.

Radio legend Dallas Wayne visits with Becky Hobbs and me backstage

Moe, Narvel Felts, Bobby Bare and T. Graham Brown, March 2009

Former band members Richard Hill and Bill Bowers

Watching Whitey Shafer perform

Tanya Tucker and I showing our love to Whitey Shafer

Thanking Tanya Tucker for coming to my benefit for Whitey Shafer.

Photo courtesy, Jerry Overcast

Jerry Overcast
© 3-18-2015

On an Alaskan cruise with Keith Bilbrey

Wearing the same shirt as Jimmy Capps by accident

With my dear friends Jimmy and Michele Capps.

Celebrating Christmas with my family

With all of my grandkids and great grandson

My great grandson Gatlin watches me from the front row

When my entire family sits down for dinner

Gene Watson, John Conlee, Moe, William Lee Golden

My wife Tami and I at The Grand Ole Opry

With my display at The Heart of Texas Country Music Museum

My children and grandchildren. Bryson, Adolph, Gracie, Lisa, Brittany, Chelsea, Laura, Mark, Ronnie, Shelby and Cameron

Honored by this marker in my hometown.

he sang "Bandy the Rodeo Clown" with me. And when some of the other residents started talking a little loud, just like he used to do at our pickin' parties, he shouted, "Red light!"

I started laughing as I thought, "There's my man right there." That was the last time I saw him alive.

Coach Royal died on November 7, 2012. Of course, we knew it was coming. He had been in bad shape. It wasn't a big shock. But it still broke my heart when he died. He had so much influence on me.

Coach Royal just inspired me so much. He was a heck of a guy. He always told me, "If you have a problem, anything at all, all you have to do is call, and I'll be there for you." Did Coach really mean that? Oh yeah. He proved it... when he saved my life.

HERE I AM, DRUNK AGAIN

If I'd done all the things I sing about, I'd be dead.

I sang about a lot of wild stuff. There was a lot of drinkin', fighting and cheatin' in my songs. If I'd have done all the cheatin' I sang about, I'd have probably been shot! Fighting? Yeah, I more than lived up to all the fightin' I sang about. And drinking? Yes, I also lived up to the drinkin'. Yeah, I did do all the drinkin' that I sang about… and a whole lot more.

One night, I had been out drinking until about 3:00 in the morning. And when I came home, I was pretty out of it. I parked in the garage, went inside and went to bed. Later that morning, my wife started yelling for me to come out to the garage. She pointed at the car and said, "Exactly how did you do this?!"

And the car was completely sideways in the garage! There wasn't any room to move it forward or back! It took a long time to finally get it out. I have no idea how I drove it in there like that.

I can look back and laugh at that now… but soon after that incident, my alcohol consumption was no laughing matter.

I had a drinkin' problem.

And it kept getting worse and worse. I kept drinking more and more. I knew I had a problem. But the funny thing was, everyone around me kept telling me that I didn't have a problem. I did my shows. I never missed a concert, and I never walked onstage when I was drunk. But I would party down with anyone after every show.

I mentioned that everyone kept telling me I was OK and that I didn't have the problem, but there was one person who was able to see that I was in trouble. It was one my best friends, Mel Tillis. Mel is one of the funniest guys onstage, and he's even funnier when he's offstage. Mel used to call me, "Bambi." He'd hug my neck and stutter, "Now B-B-Bambi… you, you, you need to quit drinkin' that whiskey. You need to just drink beer."

I'd tell him, "But Mel, I love it."

He'd insist, "Bambi, listen to me... you, you, you need to stop the whiskey."

I love Mel.

I was attending Darrell Royal's retirement party in Dallas. As I walked through the hotel lobby, I heard someone yell out my song, "Here I Am, Drunk Again!" I turned around and I saw Mickey Mantle! Mickey was dealing with the same drinking problem that I was, and he told me that he loved my song, "Here I Am, Drunk Again."

For many years, I never tried to quit drinkin'. I never wanted to stop. And when the time finally came that I tried to quit, I found that I couldn't. I was really addicted to booze. I was drinking more whiskey every day, and I just got to a point where I was in bad shape.

I was flying on Southwest Airlines. This was long before they had all the airplane security and laws that they have today. And I was drunker than a skunk, as I sat in the middle seat between two people. I was in a pretty lousy mood, since I had this crummy seat. And my drinking wasn't helping anything.

In the middle of the flight, I spilled a drink on the guy next to me. He started yelling at me. He called me "a damn drunk", and I just hit him as hard as I could. When we landed in Houston, the police were waiting on me. But one of them was a big fan of mine, and they let me go. These days, they would probably have to put me in jail.

In 1983, I got a call from a man in Hollywood, who told me a gal was making a movie and she wanted to go out on the road with me. She thought that that would help her with her part in the film. It turned out to be the great actress Ellen Barkin. She was going to star in a movie called "Tender Mercies."

Ellen met me in San Antonio. She had an aunt who lived there, and we took Ellen out on tour with us. She rode on my bus for four or five days. One night, Ellen took a bottle of whiskey and sat it on the table, and we polished it off as we talked through the evening. She slept on one of the top bunks of the bus. I had a sound guy, and one night he started climbing up to her bunk. Ellen hit him and knocked him clear across the aisle.

I was pretty surprised and honored that she would want to shadow me on the road... until she told me the reason. She had wanted to know what it was like in real life, because in the movie, she portrayed a woman who was in love with "a broken down, alcoholic singer"!

Lucky Me by Moe Bandy

Robert Duvall ended up winning the Academy Award for "Tender Mercies." He was the one who played the broken down, alcoholic singer. I'd met him when we played at Billy Bob's. He might have been studying me that night, too.

You know you have to be a pretty bad alcoholic if Hollywood wants to use you as an example! A broken down, alcoholic singer. That's pretty rough. I wasn't broken down, but I sure was broken. And I sure was an alcoholic.

In the summer of 1983, I hit possibly the lowest point in my life. Now, almost thirty-five years later, it is still hard for me to talk about it. But I will.

I got into a very serious fight, and this time, I came out on the losing end. I ended up with a concussion and broken ribs. I also tore the cruciate ligament in my leg. It just blew out my knee. I would have to have surgery. And I would be on crutches as I recovered.

As I dealt with my physical injuries, I was also going through a lot of mental pain. Some people had been making up stories about me that were completely untrue. They were totally made up. But to know that someone would spread such rumors, and to know that some of my fans were believing those stories, just devastated me.

I was so depressed. I thought my career was over. I was miserable. I decided to get a room at a hotel in Seguin, Texas, and I took a gun with me. I was really close to ending it all. I knew that alcoholism had taken control of my life. That night, alone in that hotel room, I came very close to taking my own life.

But for some reason, instead of picking up my gun, I picked up my wallet. And Coach Darrell Royal's name and number fell out onto the nightstand. I dialed his number, and when he answered, I said, "Coach, I am messed up bad."

He asked me where I was, and then he told me, "Hold on. Don't do anything."

The next thing I know, he is standing at my door.

Coach got me dressed, and put me in his car. Then he drove me to the airport and we got on a plane headed for Orange County, California. As soon as we boarded, I told the stewardess, "I want every drink that you have ever mixed in your life. I want to drink them one after another."

The stewardess looked at Coach, and he said, "OK. No problem. Bring 'em on." And they brought me every alcoholic drink that they had on that plane. And I drank every one of them.

When we landed, I could barely walk, as Coach Royal led me off the plane. Coach knew the head of a drug and alcohol treatment center. He took me out there, and he stayed with me for five days, just to make sure I was OK. I stayed at that treatment center for twenty-one days... I would not have done it for anyone else. I would not have gone with anyone, except Coach Royal. He truly saved my life.

When I first began my stay in the treatment center, they put me in a room with a guy who was hooked on heroin. Of course, I was used to having the "star suite." I wasn't pleased that I had to share a room with anyone, let alone a heroin junkie. I was still on my crutches after my knee surgery, so when my "roommate" started moaning and groaning, I yelled, "Hey partner! You had better stop that shit. Or I will come over there and whip your ass with my crutch!"

Coach Royal's wife Edith also played a big role in my recovery. Edith was very involved in alcohol and drug treatment programs and she was familiar with the treatment center in California. She was a very big help to me during that entire period. And Edith became known for her advocacy of drug and alcohol rehabilitation. Today you can find the Edith Royal Campus at Austin Recovery, the substance abuse treatment center in Austin Texas.

♬

Larry Gatlin is one of my best friends. At the time, Larry was going through the same stuff I was, and he also happened to be friends with Coach Royal. When I came back home, Larry asked me, "How do you feel?"

I said, "I feel really good." And Coach Royal ended up taking Larry to the very same treatment center.

I stopped drinking alcohol when I was forty years old. And I haven't had a drink for more than thirty years. That day when I drank everything on the plane was the last day I ever touched any kind of alcohol.

When I look back on that sad day when I was alone in that hotel room, I know I was at the end of my rope. And at just the moment when I was thinking that my life was over, that's when God said, "Not yet. You still have a lot of good things to do. The best part of your life is still to come."

When I first stopped drinking, I will admit that it was rough. It was very rough. There were many times when I'd get the urge to have a drink, and I'd have to call Coach Royal, and he would always be able to talk me out of it. I still had to play the clubs and bars where everyone was drinking. And my band was still drinking too.

I told them, "If you guys want to drink, please go ahead and drink. I can't hide from it." In a way, I think that kind of helped me. I had alcohol all around me. But I knew that it was not an option for me anymore. I can't ever think, "Maybe I'll have just one drink." I know I can't do it. If I would start drinking, it would end my career. It would end my family. It would end my marriage. It would be a nightmare.

I successfully quit drinking, but there was another bad habit that I had a tough time kicking: I smoked.

I started smoking when I was very young. And again, it was Coach Royal who helped me stop. Each time we would meet to play golf, Coach would say, "You need to get rid of those damn cigarettes," and I always told him, "OK Coach, I'm gonna quit." But I didn't know if I ever could.

But the day finally came, during a tour of Europe. I was smoking those bad English cigarettes, and on my way to the airport to come back home, I told myself, "This is it. I am going to stop smoking." I got on the plane, and they were going to put me in the non-smoking section. I told the stewardess, "No, no, no. I want to be in the smoking section. Because this is going to be my last fling." And I smoked one cigarette after another, all the way from Europe to Atlanta. As they opened the plane door, I put out my last cigarette, and I never touched another one again.

After I had stopped drinking and smoking, Coach Royal told me many, many times how proud he was of me. He and his wife Edith were so sweet and good to me. They really were like family to me.

After I'd quit drinking, I really wanted to be more of a family man. I wanted to be a good person. And I wanted to do something with my life that would truly make a difference in the lives of other people. Yes, I was proud of my country music career. And I knew that my music had touched many people. But I wanted to do more… something really important.

So I met with a guy named Kenny Leonard in San Antonio. Kenny owns the L & M Packing Company. It's one of the biggest meat distributers in the world. And I told him that I wanted to do something for children. I wanted to find a way that I could help kids.

Kenny and I went to the Santa Rosa Children's Hospital, and we asked them if there was anything we could do to help them. They introduced us to Sara Sutton and her husband, who had a child who had needed an organ transplant. But they couldn't get it, and their child died. So the couple wanted to start an organization that would help get children's transplants.

So together, we started The Children's Transplant Association. And I began hosting a huge golf tournament. We had every big-name entertainer come play in the tournament every year. Glen Campbell, Roy Clark and The Gatlins all came almost every year. And we raised a lot of money. I put on that tournament for nineteen years.

While I don't have the golf tournament anymore, our Children's Transplant Association is still going today. And I am so proud of that. I was also very proud when they told me that I was going to be honored for my children's charity work. I won the American Spirit Award from the Ladies Auxiliary of the VFW. Bob Hope had won the same award for his charity work, so I was very honored to be in such great company. They flew me to Las Vegas on August 22, 1989, to present me with the award.

Two years later, I was also honored with a huge award in Los Angeles. I was surprised when Dwight Yoakam introduced me as the World's Children's Transplant Humanitarian of the Year. As he introduced me, he said, "When I get through with my career, I hope that I have done as much as Moe Bandy. He has helped so many people."

To be completely honest, I had never been that big a fan of Dwight Yoakam. For some reason, when he started out, I thought he was kind of stuck up. But as he introduced me, with each great thing he said about me, the more I started liking him!

Each year at our golf tournaments, we would bring in kids who had received organ transplants. They would introduce the kids, and they'd come up onstage and hug me. Many called me their "angel." I was always so happy to see a child we had helped save. But it was also very sad when we would lose a child when their transplant didn't take and they didn't survive.

But the Children's Transplant Association is one of the things that I am the most proud of in my life. I am thankful that I helped start the

Association, and I know that there are a bunch of children who received a transplant and they are now grown men and women. They are now living normal lives, thanks to our help.

In 2017, I decided to help host a different golf tournament for another worthy cause. We held the event in October in Victoria, Texas, and we hope to build the tournament up into a real big thing. It raises money for the Blue Bonnet Ranch in Victoria, who take in abused and abandoned children and care for them.

I played in a golf tournament that was a fundraiser for the ranch, and they asked me to become the sponsor of the event. Allen Shamblin is the tournament's co-sponsor. Allen is one of the great songwriters in Nashville. He's written big hits for Randy Travis, Keith Urban, Mark Wills and Miranda Lambert.

Before I committed to sponsoring the tournament, I wanted to visit the ranch to meet the children there. Over the years, I have learned a little bit of magic, and I did a few little tricks for the kids. I poured sugar in my hand, and then made it disappear. The children loved my magic. I knew I had won them over when they started yelling, "Do that again!"

As I look back, I remember how Coach Darrell Royal had had to convince me to go golfing with him for the first time. If I hadn't gone golfing with Coach that day, I would never have fallen in love with the game, and I would never have started my golf tournament that helped us raise the millions of dollars that helped save the lives of so many children. Yeah, I'm glad I went golfing with Coach that day.

I can also say that I have been able to golf with some of the biggest legends of the sport, and that I became friends with many of those legends. One of those was Doug Sanders. Doug was a great golfer. I played in his tournament many times, and he played in mine quite a few times. I also played with, and got to know, Ben Crenshaw. In 1995, Ben was getting ready for the Masters Golf Tournament, when he called and invited me to come to the Masters as his guest. But I couldn't get away from my theater, so I had to tell him no. Ben went on to win the Masters that year and I missed it!

I once played in a game in Palm Springs, California with Arnold Palmer, Lee Trevino and Mark O'Meara. That was such a thrill! But I was so scared, as I got ready to drive off the tee with Arnold Palmer and Lee Trevino watching me. When I went to make my second shot, I looked over and saw Arnold Palmer leaning up against my golf cart. I thought, "Oh my God." Talk about pressure! But I ended up hitting a really good shot. I turned to Arnold and said, "Yeah, that's the way I always used to hit 'em." He just smiled. He was a very nice, gracious man. Just a really nice guy.

I also played golf with actor James Garner. James and I became very close friends, and we played a lot of golf together. And of course I have played a lot of golf over the years with my country music friends, like Glen Campbell, Larry Gatlin, Mickey Gilley and Johnny Lee.

BRANSON

The Roy Clark Celebrity Theatre opened in Branson, Missouri in 1983. If any big-name country artists played in Branson during that time, that was the theatre where they played. Roy didn't actually own the theatre, but they used his name.

Boxcar Willie was the first major country entertainer to buy and open a theater in Branson. Boxcar never had any hit songs, but he was such a terrific entertainer that the audiences just fell in love with him. He was so great that he became a member of the Grand Ole Opry even without having a hit record.

Boxcar played the character of a hobo. He wore overalls, and had a scruffy beard. But when Boxcar started his theater in 1985, he hit a gold mine! He made so much money that, in addition to his beautiful theater, he also opened a museum and two motels!

When Mel Tillis saw the money that Boxcar was making, he decided to move to Branson too. Many people don't know this about Mel, but he was his own manager. He had such a huge career. He recorded so many hit songs, he was one of the all-time great songwriters. He was also an actor, and of course there was no live performer who was any better. And he did it all without a manager!

Mickey Gilley quickly followed Mel to Branson, and Jim Stafford and Ray Stevens soon followed. I was also playing in Branson through the 1980s. I did my shows at the Lowes Theater. They'd bring in different entertainers, and I'd usually play two or three days at a time. When I was there, I could see the traffic and the tourists, and I had no doubt that Branson was on the verge of becoming something very great. I talked to Mel Tillis, and Mel said, "M-M-Moe, you need to come to Branson. We are making money hand over… foot!"

I had been touring big time in the late 80s. I was doing two-hundred concerts a year, and I was looking for a break from the road. After my conversation with Mel, I went to visit Mickey Gilley, and Mickey said the same thing Mel did: "Man, I'm making a killing in Branson."

I had a friend named Mac Stringfellow, who had made it big in the oil business. He was one of the nicest gentlemen I've ever been around. And he was honest, too. When Mac told you he'd do something, he did it. Mac wanted to partner with me to open a club in San Antonio where I lived, but I asked him if he had ever checked out Branson. He said, "No, but we sure can."

Mac and I flew to Branson on his private plane, and it didn't take us very long to make a decision. We bought a theater that had belonged to the Plummer family, tore it down, and totally rebuilt it. And in 1991, I opened the Moe Bandy Americana Theatre. It was absolute perfect timing. Because the Branson boom was about to hit!

Shortly after my theater opened, the national newspaper 'USA Today' put a photo of me on the cover of the paper. In the photo, I was standing in front of my new theater. On December 8, 1991, the popular TV show "60 Minutes" did an in-depth feature story about Branson, and the legendary TV reporter Morley Shafer came there to interview all of us. He talked to us while we were playing golf. "60 Minutes" called Branson "The live music capital of the universe." And after that aired on TV, it was Katy, bar the door! People were coming to Branson by the thousands.

"Branson exploded." That is the only way I can describe it after the "60 Minutes" piece aired on national TV. The town just exploded. You couldn't move. Traffic was bumper-to-bumper. You couldn't get a hotel room. You couldn't get a seat at a concert unless you booked them many months in advance. It was crazy.

Everybody in the world was coming to see our shows. I looked down from the stage one night, and there was Buddy Ebsen (Jed Clampett and Barnaby Jones) in the front row! The great actress Diane Carroll came to see us. I was always surprised to see some famous person come to our show.

But there were two visitors who I will always remember... we had a family come through town. They had a little boy who was sick. They were trying to get to Disney World, but they had only made it to Branson before they ran out of money. I ended up paying for their trip to Disney.

The other was a little girl, she was a teenager who had cancer. She was staying at a hotel by the Grand Palace. Her family had tickets to my show, but the girl was so sick that she couldn't leave her room. When I heard about it, as soon as I'd finished my concert, I took my entire band and we went and knocked on her door. We sat in her room and sang to her.

As we visited, the girl told me how much she loved all the entertainers. She said that Barbara Mandrell was her all-time favorite. Barbara was also playing in Branson, and the girl's family also had tickets for her show, but she was going to miss that one too. When the band and I left, I went to the theater where Barbara was playing, went backstage, and I asked her, "Barbara, would you do me a favor?" I explained everything, and she went with me to visit the young girl. The girl passed away a week later. I will never forget her. And I will never forget Barbara Mandrell's kindness.

You wouldn't think that anything real crazy would ever happen during our shows in Branson. We were inside a beautiful theater. The audience was an older, more mature crowd. There was no alcohol allowed. But even with all of that, we did have a few interesting things happen during a few of my Branson concerts.

Johnny Lee jumped up onstage in the middle of one of my shows. He was barefooted. He told an R-rated joke. And a few people got mad about it. But I just laughed. I think you should be yourself. And Johnny was just being himself.

But Johnny was tame, compared to what happened another night. At the end of my concert, we were closing the show with "Americana", and during the song, we always boosted the music volume up real loud. We didn't know it, but an old man had fallen asleep during the show. And when that loud music started, it woke him up out of a dead sleep. And when he woke up, he had no idea where he was or what he was doing. He took a swing at the tour director, and then he came running toward the front of the stage. He was screaming at the band as loud as he could. We had no idea what was happening! We just wanted to finish the song and get off the stage before the old guy jumped up with us.

But the craziest thing that ever happened during a show in Branson was just after we got a new theater manager. They wanted to change our show up. They wanted the band to all wear matching Lawrence Welk dress suits, and they wanted to add more production, lights and smoke to the show. They wanted to make it more like a rock and roll show.

So they ended up cutting a huge hole in the middle of the stage, and they put in a hydraulic lift under the floor. That lift would bring me up from under the stage when the band introduced me. There would be smoke all around me, and they thought that that would be a lot cooler than just me walking out on stage.

Well, everything worked at rehearsals. But when it came time for the real show, the crowd got to see what a real production was! The band started my music. The curtains opened, and smoke started coming out from the floor. The trap door opened and I started rising up. It looked like the Second Coming!

Everyone was applauding, and just when I got just my head and shoulders up above the stage, the hydraulic lift stopped! It wouldn't move. I was looking around at the band. The crowd could see just my head there above the floor, and the rest of my body was still stuck below the floor! I could hear the theater manager yell for them to close the curtain. I could also hear the audience laughing their heads off… as they stared at my little head stuck in that hole. They closed the curtain, and a couple people came running to lift me up. When the curtain opened again, the crowd was on the floor laughing, and my band members could hardly play their instruments, they were laughing so hard. Yeah, we gave 'em a production.

During the Branson boom, I was doing two shows a day, six days a week. We held 800 people at the theater, and we were filling it up every show. The people were coming in droves. My business partner Mac Stringfellow and I were doing very good. He was the one who really owned the theater, and he paid me a salary. He paid me very well. In 1996, I bought the theater from Mac. I had a $50,000 a month payment, and I was still raking in a huge profit!

Before I go any farther, I need to say a little more about Mac Stringfellow. Mac was not only my business partner, but he was also my dear friend. Long before he had ever heard of Branson, Mac had made it big in the oil and cattle businesses in Texas.

Once we'd started flying back and forth to Missouri, we usually flew in Mac's private plane. He had a great pilot. But he had one problem: he had sleep apnea! And it never failed that, just when he had gotten us up in the air and gotten leveled off, he would go to sleep!

One day, we were flying over Dallas and we got into an unbelievable storm. The pilot had fallen asleep and flew us right into the storm! Everything that wasn't buckled down was flying all over the inside of that plane. It scared me to death.

Folks ask me what it was about Branson that attracted so many people. At the time, Nashville didn't have that many live music venues. The artists recorded their songs in Nashville, but they didn't perform them live there very often. Fans and tourists found out that you could enjoy live traditional country music in Branson. And we really had the best entertainment in the world.

And people came to Branson from around the world. At the time, Branson city leaders were doing everything they could to help ease the traffic congestion around town. Vehicles would be bumper-to-bumper and really come to an almost complete stop just before show time at the theaters. And with each venue now hosting breakfast, afternoon and evening shows, show time was just about all day, every day!

Branson officials could not build new roads fast enough. Sometimes the traffic would be backed up halfway to Springfield. It was pretty amazing. Traffic got so bad that I added the joke to my show, "No one comes to Branson anymore… because it's too crowded."

My steel guitar player, John, lived only a couple miles from the theater. We'd do a show at 2:00, and be finished by 4:30. John wanted to drive home for supper, but with the traffic jams, by the time he'd gotten there and grabbed something to eat, he had to turn right around and come back for the evening show. You didn't have time for a real break. My drummer Nick told me that he drank an entire six-pack of beer on his way home. I said, "You can't drink and drive!" He said he wasn't going to hurt anyone, since he never went more than one mile an hour in the bumper-to-bumper traffic.

People also came to Branson because they knew it was a place that offered very clean, family entertainment. You knew you wouldn't hear any bad words during a show in Branson. And if someone *did* say a cuss word, it usually spread across town before the day was over… and it was usually Johnny Lee who was the guy who said the bad word! I love ya Johnny.

We had so many folks who came to see us in Branson. And they were so loyal that they'd come not only every year, but sometimes two or three times a year. They came to so many shows. We had some folks from Iowa. They would drive from Iowa every other week! They'd bring me gifts, and gifts for all the band members. They were just loyal fans. And we became very good friends.

My drummer Nick Ochoa's girlfriend's parents used to come see us all the time. They saw Nick many years before Nick ever got to meet their daughter. He ended up meeting her after a show, and they got their picture taken together. So he met his girlfriend, because her parents always came to see us.

We had a house behind the Americana Theatre, and my manager lived in the house. He called me one day and said, "There are some people here, and they say they are going to do a movie. They want to talk to you about filming it at the theater." I drove to the theater and I met Sybil Robson Orr. Sybil was the film producer. She was also a niece of Walmart founder Sam Walton.

Sybil explained that they were making a movie called "Gordy." It was about a pig! And they asked me if I could get some Branson entertainers to appear in the movie, so I went around town and got Mickey Gilley, Jim Stafford, Roy Clark, Boxcar Willie, Christy Lane, and just about every big name in Branson.

In the movie, we were all onstage singing, as we tried to raise money to find this pig named Gordy. We filmed the concert scenes at my theater, but they also built a big set in Hollywood where all the backstage scenes were filmed. It was really neat. Doug Stone was the star of the movie. He was very hot at the time, with his song "Better Off in a Pine Box." And he did a really good job in the movie. Doug is also a real good guy.

"Gordy" turned out to be a really nice movie. It debuted in theaters on May 12, 1995. But that summer, there was also another pig movie, called "Babe." Pigs were hot that year! "Babe" was nominated for seven Academy Awards. "Gordy" didn't get nominated for anything. But while it might not have won any awards, it was a nice family movie.

CHANGES

In 1986, my phone started ringing off the hook with people saying that a famous author had put me in his new book. I had no idea what they were talking about. But Stephen King had just released his horror novel called "It."

In the book, King wrote about a guy who "liked ole Moe Bandy." The guy is listening on a jukebox to some Moe Bandy songs. Then he goes upstairs and kills himself!

I had never met Stephen King. I still haven't. And I had no idea why he chose to put me in his book. But I heard that he was a fan of my music, so he wrote me in there. I was so flattered that he did that, even though the guy killed himself over me! They also made a movie from the book "It." But they didn't include the scene with the guy listening to my songs on the jukebox.

In the mid-80s, I wanted to cut some songs that were a little bit different. And I started recording a few more serious songs than the Moe and Joe stuff. I was proud of the new sound, but Rick Blackburn from CBS Records came to me and asked, "Who do you think you are, Steve Wariner or somebody?"

A short time later, in 1985, CBS dropped me from their label. I actually found out about that on the street. They let me go and they didn't even bother to tell me! When I heard, I called Rick Blackburn. I wanted to tell him off. But I was too devastated to yell. It just broke my heart. I felt bad. But I would soon be in good company.

Less than a year after I was let go, Rick Blackburn did the unthinkable: he dropped Johnny Cash from Columbia Records. Johnny had sold tens of millions of records for the company! He had been with them for twenty-six years.

Mel Tills was also dropped by his record label, so I called him to ask for his advice. After our conversation, Mel told people, "Moe called me. And he was so p-p-pitiful. I felt so sorry for him. He was just p-p-pitiful."

Mel, Johnny and I were just three of the older artists who were let go during that time. I say "older artists", but I was only forty-one years old!

As I look back on this time, I know that it was a true turning point in my life. It is the moment where my career could have come to an end. I could have chosen to listen to Rick Blackburn. But I didn't. Rick and CBS Records thought I was finished. But I knew I wasn't. They had no idea that my greatest success was still to come. They couldn't imagine that I had not yet recorded my biggest hits and my most important songs.

I think that my release from CBS made me even more determined to get back on top of the country music charts. I knew that I still had that same fire in my belly that I'd had when I first started recording.

So I called an old friend named Woody Bowles. I had given Woody one of his first jobs when he got out of college. He'd done PR and media work for me, but now he was getting into managing artists. I called him, and told him I had an artist for him to manage... me. I told him that I didn't want to quit. I wanted to get another major label deal and I wanted to have more hits.

Woody and I spent a year looking for songs. We searched for the very best songs that we could find. At the time, Woody was managing Michael Johnson. Michael had some pop hits, and when we met, he said: "I've got a song that doesn't fit me. But it fits you."

I told him, "Well, I've got a song that I think will fit you, so maybe we can swap." The song I gave him was about baseball. It was called "Diamond Dreams." Michael was from Minnesota, and that year, the Minnesota Twins went on to the World Series. And he was able to sing his song at the ball games. And the song that he gave me was "Till I'm Too Old to Die Young." It turned out to be a pretty good swap for both of us.

We were finding some great songs to record, but it was a long year. I was used to being on the radio. For the past ten years, I had always had a hit song on the radio. Almost every week, I would have a new song that was going up the Billboard charts at the same time that my latest hit was beginning to come down.

Now that I had taken an entire year off from recording, I really didn't know if I would ever be able to get back on the radio. When you are out a while, a lot of times you are finished. Most of the time, once your hits stop, especially for more than a year, it is very rare that you can start having hits again.

In the summer of 1986, we met Dick Whitehouse. Dick was with MCA/Curb Records, and on July 4th, in front of a crowd of 51,000 people at a concert in Oklahoma, I signed my new record deal with Curb. We signed the contract onstage. It was sort of my own Declaration of Independence.

That following winter, on January 12, 1987, MCA/Curb released my new album, very fittingly titled, "You Haven't Heard the Last of Me." The first single from the album was "Till I'm Too Old to Die Young." We followed that up with the title song from the album. And just after "You Haven't Heard the Last of Me" became a big hit, I happened to run into my old pal Rick Blackburn from CBS. Rick quietly told me, "I got the message."

I owe a lot of my comeback to Woody Bowles. He was a great help to me. Woody not only managed me, but he also played a big role in Ricky Skaggs' career. And he managed Terri Clark, and also another act that you might have heard of, called The Judds. I was one of the first people to ever hear The Judds.

One day, Woody and I got caught in a snow storm in Nashville. As we sat in traffic, he said, "I want you to listen to this." And he put a tape in his player.

It was Wynonna and Naomi Judd singing "Mama, He's Crazy." It was just them along with a guitar. Woody asked, "What do you think of a mother and daughter act?"

I said, "Well, the Kendalls were big with a father and daughter. But a mother and daughter? I don't know if that would work or not."

Woody sighed, "Well, I've got 'em. We just cut this. And the daughter is staying at my house, because she's not getting along with her mom!"

Of course, the entire world would soon meet The Judds. And we all soon found out that yes, a mother and daughter act could indeed work!

THE PRESIDENT IS CALLING

In 1980, I was in Wichita, Kansas when I got a call from one of President Jimmy Carter's staff members. They said, "President Carter is going to be in Fort Worth, and he would like to have you there. We can send a plane to come get you."

I said, "Well, I'm votin' for Reagan." But then I thought a second, and said, "Hey, this is the President of the United States. And if he wants me, then I will be there."

The President gave a speech in front of the Fort Worth Stockyard steps, and I stood right next to him. When he got through, the secret service came to me and said, "The President would like for you to ride to the airport in his car." I got in the limo with Mr. Carter. Billy Bob Burnette, the man who created the Billy Bob's club, was also in the car. Our limo passed right by the big warehouse that Billy Bob had just bought, and he pointed out the window and said, "Mr. President, the World's Biggest Honky Tonk is going to be right there. And I'm the guy who's building it." Less than a year later, on April 1, 1981, "Billy Bob's" 'the World's Biggest Honky Tonk' was opened.

When we got to the airport, President Carter asked us, "Would you guys take a picture with me?" I couldn't believe it! The President of the United States was asking to get his photo with us! I said, "Of course we would!" President Carter was a big fan of country music. I didn't agree with his politics at all. But he was a good man.

One of my biggest hits was released in January of 1988. It was called "Americana." It was a song saluting small-town America, old-fashioned ways and values. "Americana" touched the hearts of so many people... including the President of the United States.

George H.W. Bush was running for President in 1988. He had been Vice President under Ronald Reagan for the past eight years. My manager got a phone call from Mr. Bush's campaign manager, and they said, "We are playing Moe's song 'Americana' on Mr. Bush's campaign bus tours, and we were wondering if Moe would like to come out and be with us." I jumped at the chance!

I was already a big Republican. I was a fanatic conservative. They flew me and my band to Chicago, and when I got there, they sat me down in a campaign bus. I was startled when the secret service guys burst in. Then here comes Mr. Bush and his wife Barbara. He gave me a huge smile, stuck out his hand and said, "Hello Moe! How are you doin'? I'm a huge fan!" We ended up doing eight rallies in different towns that first day.

They had a string of buses, and I rode on the bus with the Bushes. We had lunch together on the bus. I was able to get so close to them. They are just the greatest folks in the world. I would go out and sing "Americana", and then a few minutes later, Mr. Bush would come out. But later in the day, Mr. Bush asked, "Would you like to bring me on?"

So I sang my song, and then I said, "Ladies and Gentlemen, the next President of the United States, George Bush!"

At the end of the day, almost as soon as I got home, my phone rang. They asked, "Would you like to do that again?"

I said, "Put me down for everything you've got."

They flew me to Cincinnati to meet the tour. Mr. Bush was getting really hot by then, and it looked like he was going to win the election easily.

When I got to Cincinnati, they put me in a little trailer house. And all of a sudden, here comes the Vice President and all of his entourage. They were all in this little trailer with me. Mr. Bush said, "Moe, help me put this thing on." And I helped him put on his bulletproof vest. I zipped it up for him, then we met the Cincinnati Reds star, Johnny Bench, and me, Johnny and George Bush all got onto a fire truck. The three of us rode through downtown Cincinnati on that truck, and it was like a ticker tape parade, with confetti falling down on us. Mr. Bush joked that all of the people might have turned out to cheer on Johnny Bench and not him. I was just excited to be there. When we got to the rally, I sang "Americana" and introduced Mr. Bush. That was one of the biggest thrills of my life.

John Clark, my fiddle player, also went with me on a lot of the campaign stops. One day, we were eating lunch in a high school gymnasium. It was really crowded, and John had to stand up while he ate. He was holding his plate, when Mr. Bush saw him. Mr. Bush asked,

"Where is John's seat?" When no one moved, the Vice President said, "Well, I'm not going to eat until he does." He yelled, "Hey John! Come over here and sit by me! And John ended up sitting right between George and Barbara Bush!

John also got the Presidential treatment at another rally. He and I were getting off the Vice President's bus. John was playing fiddle and mandolin, and he was carrying both of them as he walked off of the bus. But Mr. Bush grabbed his mandolin and said, "Here, I'll carry that."

I saw it and said, "It looks like you've got a pretty good roadie there, John!"

On October 29, 1988, I appeared at a Bush rally in Crystal Lake, Illinois. Crystal Gayle and her sister Peggy Sue were also with us. By then, Loretta Lynn, Crystal and Peggy were touring with us. Our bus tours got a whole lot funner when Loretta, Crystal and Peggy signed on. They would all sing, and then I would sing. It was great. And the rallies all got a lot bigger as Election Day got closer. We were doing rallies all over the country. Everywhere Mr. Bush campaigned, we were there too. It was so much fun.

As the campaign wrapped up, we wondered where our last rally would be. And Mr. Bush told us, "I am going to close this run in Houston. I want Moe Bandy to sing "Americana" one more time, and that's the way we're going to end our campaign."

At the final campaign event, the Texas Governor gave a speech, and some senators also talked. Then they announced me. They started the track for my song "Americana." I had a tape of the music, but I sang live to it. But as soon as the music started, the tape stopped. I looked to the side of the stage, and saw Mr. Bush standing there. I had no idea what to do. They couldn't get my music going.

Right then, Loretta Lynn and Crystal Gayle both ran out onstage. Loretta hugged me and she was laughing. And right then, we decided to sing "God Bless America." We didn't have any music. But we didn't need any. We just sang it, and everyone in the crowd sang along.

When I got home that night, my phone rang. It was George Bush. He said, "Moe, I felt so bad about what happened to your music." I couldn't believe he was calling. Here he was, on the night before the biggest day of his life, and he was concerned about me! He said, "Why don't you come back down and be with me when the votes come in tomorrow?"

I said, "Sure! That would be an honor."

And I was sitting with George and Barbara Bush and their family when the votes were counted. I was in the room when he learned that he would be the next President of the United States. What a thrill it was to be there at that historic time.

On January 20, 1989, I performed for Mr. Bush at the Presidential Inauguration. Randy Travis, Lee Greenwood, The Oak Ridge Boys, Loretta Lynn and Crystal Gayle all performed as well. Yes, George Bush was a fan of country music!

I was also invited to play at a little party at the White House. President Bush always told everyone, "This guy had a lot to do with me becoming President and being here in the White House." I was so honored. I couldn't believe the President was saying that.

The President called me on another occasion. He asked, "Hey Moe, what are you doing Wednesday?"

I said, "I guess nothing Sir."

He said, "Come on up to the White House. I've got a golf outing and I'd like you to be a part of it."

So I flew to Washington, D.C.

They picked me up at the airport and took me to the White House. This seems so hard to believe as I look back on it, but it really happened. They were having a cabinet meeting when I got there. And President Bush saw me and said, "Come on in, Moe! We are just wrapping this up!" I sat at the big table with his cabinet. The President introduced me to everyone.

Then we went to have lunch. President Bush whispered, "I've got you a couple golfing partners. And they are pretty good." It turned out to be Lee Trevino and Doug Sanders, two of the greatest golfers ever. Lee, Doug, President Bush, and me, that was the foursome. We played eighteen holes of golf. Every time we'd hit the ball, a secret service guy would be right on top of it, showing you where it landed.

When we finished our golf, we went back to the White House. I had also brought a couple of my band members with me, and we played music for everyone. At the end of the night, just before I headed to bed, the First Lady, Barbara, said, "Moe, let's go for a walk."

The President said, "Barbara and I like to walk outside in the evening, and sometimes we'll go down to the fence to surprise the tourists." And that's exactly what we did. Lee Trevino, Doug Sanders, the President, the First Lady, and I all walked down to the White House gate. And it was here that something happened that I will never forget as long as I live: as we got closer to the gate, there were two college kids standing on the other side. As they watched us all walk toward them, one of them yelled out, "Hey, there's Moe Bandy!" The President got a big laugh out of that.

President Bush invited me to come up to Camp David for a weekend with him. I took my sixteen-year-old daughter Lisa with me, and we had so much fun. We played a game called Wallyball, where you hit a ball against a wall. Lisa played on the President's team, and I was on the other team. We also played horseshoes. As we were playing, I looked up to see a golf cart just flying down the hill toward us. Barbara Bush was in the passenger seat, and my daughter was driving! A couple of Barbara's grandkids were in the back, holding on for dear life. Lisa was going so fast, and I thought "Oh my God, she is going to turn that thing over and kill the First Lady!"

But the most surprising thing that we did that weekend was shooting skeet. I was standing right next to the President as I held a loaded shotgun! The Secret Service was right on top of me the whole time. They didn't take their eyes off of me, and they would only give me one shell at a time! Finally, President Bush told them, "Oh, let him fill up his gun!"

I sang at their private chapel during the church service. Afterward, at Sunday dinner, the President said, "I want Lisa sittin' next to me." That totally thrilled my daughter. During the meal, he told her, "I want to hear about the East Central High School that you go to." Then he wrote a note to excuse her from school for the days she missed that week. On the note, the President handwrote, "Lisa was a good girl at Camp David."

That night, we watched a couple movies with the President and First Lady. One of the movies was "Edward Scissorhands." I don't remember what the other one was. Before the movie started, Mr. Bush told my daughter, "Lisa, you sit over here by me." He really gave her the Presidential treatment, and I will always be grateful to him.

The next day, Lisa and I got on a plane to head home. I happened to get a seat next to a well-known movie critic, and when I saw him, I said, "I saw a great movie last night. It was 'Edward Scissorhands'."

He said, "You didn't see that movie. It's not out yet."

I said, "I saw it. I was with the President. He had an advance copy." I always liked to shut up any critic!

President Bush liked my traditional country music. He really liked it. But he was a big fan of all country music. One day, we were sitting together, and he asked me, "What is George Strait like?"

I answered, "He's a good guy."

He said, "I would really like to meet him someday."

I laughed, "Well, he'd probably like to meet you too!"

Not long after, not only did the two Georges meet, but they became very good friends.

♫

During one of my visits to the White House, I was in my room on the phone talking with my mother when the President walked in. He asked, "Who's on the phone?"

"My mother," I replied.

He grabbed the phone from me and said, "Mrs. Bandy, Moe is sure being a good boy up here at the White House."

President Bush went on a hunting trip outside Alice, Texas. While he was there, his family planned a special surprise party for him. He knew nothing about the party, but Mrs. Bush had asked me to come sing at it, so they hid me backstage, and my band got set up before Mr. Bush came in. But as they walked him to his seat, the President looked up at the stage and yelled, "That's Moe Bandy's band!" Of course, all of my band members were thrilled that the President of the United States knew them!

In August of 1990, President Bush was trying to deal with Saddam Hussein. I happened to be with the President at Camp David when Operation Desert Storm was getting ready to begin. I will never forget how Mr. Bush came to me and said, "We're gonna light 'em up tonight Moe."

In the summer of 1992, I was having dinner with the President, when he leaned over and said, "Tell us about this Branson place. What's going on down there?"

I started off by saying, "Well, it's down in the Ozarks, and it is just amazing."

The President said, "We are going to come see you one of these days."

I excitedly said, "Boy, wouldn't that be a thrill."

A few months later, the President called me and said, "I'm going to have my people get in touch with you. Would you sing at the Republican National Convention in Houston?"

I quickly answered, "Yes sir. I'd be honored."

Then, kind of as an afterthought, he said, "By the way, when we leave the National Convention, we are coming to see you in Branson."

I yelled into the phone, "Are you kiddin' me?!"

He laughed, "No, we're comin'. I want you to call a press conference, and you tell them that YOU are bringing me there. I want you to get all the credit for it."

I said, "Oh my God, what a deal."

So I called a big press conference. All the TV, radio and newspaper people were there, and when I announced, "I am bringing the President of the United States to Branson, Missouri," everyone just sat there stunned. They were speechless!

And when I said, "He is coming to my theater to see my show," man, I was the buzz. Everybody was talking about Moe Bandy, and how in the world did he pull this off!

Before the visit, I had to arrange for a place for the President and all of the people he needed to stay, so I called the Palace Hotel. They were about the fanciest place in town, and I thought they would have more rooms than anybody. But when I told them that I needed sixty-five rooms, the guy at the desk said, "Are you kidding me?!" This was right in the middle of the busiest tourist season. Just one hotel room was tough to get at the last moment, and sixty-five rooms was probably impossible. The man said, "There is just no way."

I said, "What if it was the President of the United States who needed the rooms?"

He paused a moment, and said, "Oh, let's see what we can do."

The hotel ended up taking all of their guests who had reservations and putting them into another hotel. I was relieved that I was able to pull off sixty-five rooms… relieved until I got another call from the White House. They said that the press and media also needed rooms. So I had to call the Palace back, and ask for another fifty rooms!

The Secret Service came in two weeks early, to go through the theater. And on the day of the President's visit, we also held a big rally for him at the Silver Dollar City theme park. Glen Campbell, Loretta Lynn, Tony Orlando, Boxcar Willie, Mickey Gilley, and all the big stars of Branson were at the rally. After that event, I got in the car with the President and the First Lady, and we drove toward my theater. And the entire Branson strip, the main street, was lined with people hollerin' and screamin'. I was sitting in the back of the car, feelin' like a big dog.

When we arrived at my theater, we pulled the Presidential limo right under a large awning that I had built onto the back of the theater. The awning was right by my dressing room. The President and First Lady stepped out of the car and right into my dressing room. We had a little cocktail party backstage before I went out and did my entire concert.

Loretta Lynn and Glen Campbell also came to the show. All of the politicians from around the state of Missouri were also there, along with all the local leaders. My band was so excited. A couple of them were in tears during the show, as they watched the President and First Lady enjoying themselves from their front row seats.

After the concert, President Bush came up onstage, and we sang "Americana" with Mr. and Mrs. Bush. Then they both went around and hugged each guy in my band. The President went back to Nick Ochoa, who was sitting behind his big, glass drum case. Mr. Bush had to reach way up over the drum cage, and Nick had to try to keep drumming with one hand, as he shook the President's hand with the other.

When President Bush came to my show, he and Barbara sat in the very center seats in the first row. All of the seats in the theater were blue, but we made those two seats red. And later, we took those seats out and replaced them with two others. The actual seats that the President and First Lady sat in are in the attic of that theater right now. And the current owners probably have no clue of what they are.

When I think about it, I am pretty sure that might have been the biggest day in the history of Branson. Probably the highlight of my career was playing at the White House. That was unbelievable. But having the President come all the way to Branson to MY theater just to see ME… that would have to be right up there, when it comes to the highlight of my life.

But life can be a rollercoaster. On August 21, 1992, I was with the President of the United States, enjoying one of the greatest days of my life. But, just three days later, I had one of worst. My dad died. Dad had been very sick. He had Parkinson's Disease, and was going downhill very fast. I had been going back and forth from Branson to Texas to be with him as much as I could.

Earlier in this book, I talked about my dad being pretty rough on me when I was growing up. But he had mellowed quite a bit over the years. He never said that he was sorry for the things he did back then, but I knew he was. Later in his life, I took my dad with me on a tour of Montana and Utah, and it was one of the best trips I ever took in my life. We healed a lot of stuff on that trip.

During the last year of dad's life, he couldn't talk at all. With all excitement of the President's visit to my theater, I was so proud of everything that was going on in my life, but with my dad so sick, it was all very bittersweet. Luckily, just after President Bush left Branson, I did too. I flew to Texas to be with dad, and I was holding his hand when he died. I was also with my mother when she died ten years later.

President Bush called me one day and said, "We are celebrating the 100th anniversary of our home in Kennebunkport. Can you come up for a little party?" As always, I told him that I would be honored to be there. I had been to the home once before, but I knew that this would be an even more special occasion.

I took John, my fiddle player, with me, and he brought his fiddle and guitar along. When we arrived, they said I would be staying with the Bushes in their home, but that John would be staying at a nearby hotel that was on the lake. Later that day, as I visited with the President, he suddenly said, "Let's go check on John!" He told a Secret Service agent, "We are going on the boat."

With that, some of the agents started running to get their wetsuits.

We took the boat and docked right next to the hotel. John was laying on his bed when he heard a knock on his door. And when he opened it, he was totally shocked to see President Bush standing there!

The President asked him, "How is your room?"

John said, "It's great. Thank you."

President Bush loved doing things like that.

In honor of the special occasion of the 100th anniversary of the Bush's Kennebunkport home, I wrote a song called, "This Wonderful House." When I sang it for them, they were all in tears. They just loved it. George W. was President at the time, and he ordered fifteen copies of the song. I put it down on a CD with my band. It was just a real rough cut, but it was very special to the Bush family.

During the celebration, they rented a VFW club there, and they invited everyone who had ever had anything to do with their home there. After the party, Barbara Bush said to me, "You come have a ride with me. I've got a new car." From when they were Vice President and then President and First Lady, George and Barbara had not driven a car themselves in thirteen years!

But Barbara had just bought a new SUV. She smiled and whispered, "We'll get rid of the Secret Service." She turned to one agent and said, "Don't be following me. Just leave us alone." We took off, and she was laughing the whole way.

When we got back, I asked a Secret Service guy, "Did we lose you?"

He laughed and said, "No. We always knew where you were."

The President also took me to Greece. It was one of the biggest and most memorable trips of my life. There was a man there who owned a big shipping operation, and he became very close friends with President Bush. Every year, President Bush would go to Greece for a trip on one of the man's ships. But the President's trip to Greece in 2004 would be extra special… and I would be going along!

The Summer Olympic Games were being held in Greece in 2004. President Bush wasn't about to miss that, and he called his old friend Moe Bandy to invite him on the trip! We sailed all the islands, and every day, we'd stop to walk over the different islands as we learned about the history of each one. We walked the Greek island of Patmos, where John wrote the Book of Revelation.

Then we took the ship to Athens to go to the Olympics. When everyone found out that the President was on the ship, they just went crazy. We attended the opening ceremony of the Olympic Games, and I sat next to the President. The next day, we went to the Olympic village and met a lot of the athletes.

After leaving the Olympics, we toured even more islands, and each evening, wherever we were, I would play music for everyone. I'd play my guitar and sing. The leader is Israel was there. King Albert of Monaco was there. And good ol' boy Moe Bandy was there! I still shake my head as I think back to those times. It was one of the biggest thrills of my life.

During our trip to Greece, the President and I watched a man play a unique instrument called a bouzouki. It looked like a big gourd with a neck. I casually said, "Man, I like that."

The next day, the ship captain told me that I should go to my room. When I opened my door, I saw a brand new bouzouki lying on my bed. President Bush had bought it for me! It is a gift that I will always treasure.

I also got to know the entire Bush family. I got to know the younger President Bush. I became friends with George W., and also with Jeb and Marvin Bush. I had a song called "Brotherly Love", and they always wanted me to sing it for them.

For many years, twenty or twenty-five years, I would talk on the phone with President Bush at least every two or three months. And it was always the same thing every time I answered the phone. An operator would say, "The President of the United States would like to talk to Moe Bandy."

On one of those calls, President Bush told me he had several guitars in his Presidential Library, but he wanted to put my Alvarez guitar right up front so that everyone could see it. I was very honored.

On January 10, 2009, my wife Tami and I went to the commissioning of the U.S.S. George H. W. Bush supercarrier ship. The President and Barbara invited us. We also had dinner with them the night before the ceremony. What a great honor to be there with them.

Tami and I also went to see the Bushes' a few years ago. We went to their home in Houston. What great folks. Those people, their whole family, are great Americans who wanted to help the country. I love George and Barbara Bush.

THE FALL OF BRANSON...AND OF MOE

The 1990s were good years for Moe Bandy. When I wasn't palling around with President Bush, I was playing to one sold out crowd after another in Branson. But before the decade was over, I would have to go through one of the most painful periods of my life.

In 1997, my marriage to Margaret came to an end. We had been married for thirty-three years! She had been my high school sweetheart. We were married just a year after we'd graduated high school, and we ended up seeing the world. And we ended up being friends with Presidents!

Margaret was a good woman. But she married a sheet metal worker. That's what she thought I would do for the rest of my life. But she'd ended up with a country singer. She had no idea that I was going to be a singer and, eventually, a country music star. And that caused a lot of our problems. Early in our marriage, it caused problems, because I spent every last penny that we had on my singing career. So I can understand why she didn't appreciate that.

But when my career finally started taking off, she was excited. We both were! But neither of us realized what it would do to our marriage. We didn't know that I was going to be gone on the road all the time. And when I was out on the road being a country star, she was at home trying to raise our kids. And she did a great job of doing that, mostly by herself.

♫

Another problem we had was that we both drank. We were drinkin' buddies. But then, we got to fighting when we drank. And when I quit drinking when I was forty, she didn't want to quit. She tried to hide it and do it on the side. And she did most of her drinking when I was out of town.

And as time went on, we just kind of drifted apart. We went in two different directions as we got older. And as we grew apart, we fought more. Margaret was with me for the first six years that I was in Branson.

She moved from Texas to Branson. But when we divorced, she moved back to Texas to be near our children.

As I write this book, Margaret is in very poor health. She has had six strokes, and is in a nursing home. It breaks my heart.

Owning a theater in Branson is a full-time job. We would do two shows every day, six days a week. If you got sick, you still did your show. If you have some kind of personal problem or death in the family, you know you are still expected onstage that afternoon and evening. The show would go on, no matter what! But what happens when there is a national tragedy?

On September 11, 2001, I had two shows booked at the theater. That morning, we watched the terrorists fly the planes into the Twin Towers in New York City. And as our afternoon show neared, we kept wondering what we should do. We knew that we had people who were expecting us to give them a concert.

We finally decided that we needed to go ahead with the show. We didn't want the terrorists to stop us.

We ended up having a pretty good crowd that day, but the audience was very subdued. We ended the show as always with "Americana." I think everyone was crying. We all felt very patriotic. We were also worried. There was a rumor that someone had put two bombs inside the dam on Table Rock Lake in Branson. Everyone was scared to death. But nothing ever happened.

The terrorists couldn't stop the shows in Branson, but soon, something else would cause many of the theaters to go dark forever.

Remember when I mentioned that "60 Minutes" news story? During our interview with Morley Shafer, Mel Tillis told the viewers that he was making six million dollars a year at his theater in Branson! Every entertainer, country music and otherwise, heard that comment. And that comment opened the floodgates. Everybody packed up their microphone and guitar, and headed to Branson to make their millions.

Jim Stafford came to see my show, and shortly after, he had his own theater. Tony Orlando came to visit, and soon became a Branson resident. Even 'Mr. Las Vegas', Wayne Newton, came to see our show, and you guessed it… he became 'Mr. Branson'!

Andy Williams, Willie Nelson, Glen Campbell, and even Johnny Cash all announced that they would be coming to Branson. It seemed that everybody had their own theater. The town went from having a half-dozen theatres to more than a hundred! It was nuts. And someone should have been able to see that it could not last. Of course, all of those theaters and those who owned them (Moe Bandy) started splitting the pie, the profits, into real little pieces. That six-million-dollar piece of pie Mel Tillis and Mickey Gilley once enjoyed was suddenly cut into a hundred tiny bites. Go ahead, divide $6,000,000 by 100. The answer is not pretty, when you have a $50,000 a month mortgage on your theater.

And then things got worse. Other acts started discounting their tickets through different ticket outlets. They were selling their tickets for $2.50 to $3.00 each. Of course we couldn't compete with that. Who would even want to try to compete? And of course, that was not going to work on any long-term basis for the act or theater that was doing it.

So these acts that no one had ever heard of were strutting around town, bragging that they had bigger crowds than I did. They were playing to full houses because the ticket outlets were selling their shows at a huge discount! But at my theater, I was only getting 200-300 people. And if I didn't make a deal with the ticket brokers and agree to almost give away my tickets, then any time a tourist or fan walked in and asked for a Moe Bandy ticket, they would be told that my show was sold out!

It just killed everybody. And the big-name entertainers started leaving, because they couldn't make as much money there as they could make on the road.

The bus tour operators also affected Branson in a huge way… for good and for bad. Many theaters and artists could not have stayed in business without the bus tours coming in. We were always thankful for the big bus groups. But the way that some of the tours were handled also had a negative impact.

When they sold a lot of the tours, they promoted them as "Three days in Branson and nine shows!" The people who paid their money didn't even know the concerts they were going to see. They just had to go to whatever show the tour took 'em to. A lot of them didn't even know who Moe Bandy was, but the tour buses would drag the people (most were older folks) in there. And they had been up since 5 am that morning. They'd already gone to a breakfast show. Then they had gone to an afternoon show. Then by the time they had made it to our evening show, they were all just worn out.

Oh yeah… I forgot that just before they got to our place, they had also stopped at a huge buffet for supper! Everyone was stuffed with food. And by the time I stepped out onstage, everyone was ready for a long nap! And when the lights dimmed for the show, many people actually did fall asleep! It is horrible for any artist to look out into the crowd and see people sleeping during their show. I hated it. But then I started to make a joke out of it. You had to! Sometimes I would go out into the audience and walk up to an old guy who was sleeping. I'd say, "Well, it looks like this man is enjoying our show!"

But we did make a lot of fans from the bus tours. Many hadn't heard of Moe Bandy, but after they'd seen our show, they became big fans. And they would come back to see us the next time they came to town.

Branson regulars, those fans who come every year, have wondered why the headliners seem to change to a different theater every year. Here's the answer. Whoever owns the theater (and it is usually not the star whose name is on the theater), if you do good, will start wanting more money from you to be able to play there. If you don't do well, and you don't draw a bunch of people, then the owner wants to kick you out. So you are damned if you do, and damned if you don't.

Eventually, for a lot of the big-name stars who chose to stay in Branson, even for those who had made millions of dollars during the boom, they ended up staying until all the money they'd made was gone. They ended up spending it all! It was like the old joke about the farmer who won the lottery: when a news reporter asked what he was going to do with the money, he said, "I'm just gonna keep farming until it's all gone." And I was one of those who stayed on his tractor in Branson.

And then things got worse.

I was working myself to death. I was killing myself. I was flat out killing myself. But no matter how hard I worked, I knew that I couldn't keep up with the monthly payment on my theater. But I *did* manage to get lucky when Janet Dailey, the famous romance author, paid me a visit. She lived in Branson, and she and her husband had found a female singer who they wanted to back. They came and made me an offer I couldn't refuse, and I sold them my theater.

But I still didn't have the sense to go back on the road. That's what I should have done. Instead, I chose to stay in Branson. I continued doing lots of shows there. I worked at Gilley's theater. Then, the next year, I moved across the street to another theater. I kept switching to different venues, and with each move, I learned the same lesson… that almost no one could make a living there anymore. I was trying to stay in business and keep my band going. I would do my shows, but I was losing money on each one. When we'd play to 100 or 200 people, instead of the 800 we had been playing to a few years earlier, I started to wonder, "Do they still know me out there?" It was a terrible time.

And then things got worse. Way worse.

I had a heart attack.

On December 8, 2002, I had just finished my show, signed autographs for everyone like always, and then headed home. And I started having chest pains. Like most men, I just sat there. It wasn't unbearable, and I thought, "I'll wait and see if it gets any worse." A few minutes later, it did. All of a sudden, the pain started going down my arm. I got into the car and drove to the hospital.

As soon as I got to the local Skaggs hospital, the pain seemed to go away, as they hooked my up to all their machines. I told them, "I'm sorry I bothered y'all. I'm OK now."

The ER doctor said, "No, you just had a heart attack."

As they were checking me over, my heart started fluttering, and then it stopped. A few seconds later, it started beating again. They said, "You have to have surgery right now."

I wanted to transfer to a bigger hospital in Springfield, but the doctors insisted, "You don't have time. You need to have it done right now!" and they took me to the operating room at Skaggs Regional Cardiac Center, where I underwent a four-hour triple bypass surgery.

I had to cancel all of my concerts as I recovered for the next couple of months. During that time, I wondered why I ended up with three clogged arteries. I was only fifty-eight years old. I was in good shape, and I had stopped smoking years ago, so I knew what the reason had to be.

It was all stress. Every bit of it was caused by stress. I had been worried about keeping all my people working. And it had all just come to a head. And it almost did me in.

Just after my surgery, Mel Tillis came to see me in the hospital. I told him I was worried about all of my employees since I couldn't do any shows for a while. And on his way out, he said, "Oh, I forgot to give you this." He handed me a check for $10,000. I will never, ever forget that Mel did that for me. What a great guy.

There was one other stressful thing that happened to me in Branson. It was a few years before my heart attack, during a time when I was sharing a theater with Anita Bryant. Anita was a former Miss Oklahoma. She went on to become the spokesman for Florida orange juice and she had a few hit songs, but in the 1970s, she became one of the most outspoken opponents of gay rights. Oh, and there was one more thing… in 1980, in the hit movie "Airplane", there's a scene where all the passengers get violently ill and all throw up. Leslie Nielson's character says, "I haven't seen anything like this since the Anita Bryant concert!" So that didn't help Anita's ticket sales! But she did a morning show at the same theater where I did the night show.

Anita was a nice lady, but her husband Charlie was a loudmouth blowhard. I didn't like him at all. And I couldn't name you one person in all of Branson who liked him. Charlie and Anita had hired a bunch of musicians that they didn't pay. They were also mean to them. Everybody in town was talking about them, and everybody in town was afraid of Charlie. He always bragged about being a karate expert. He also liked to drink, and he was very intimidating when he did.

One morning, I was at the theater, and we were having tryouts for a new girl singer. There were quite a few people there. All of my band was onstage. I was standing in an aisle when the side door suddenly swung open, Charlie came storming in, heading right toward me.

He yelled, "I heard what you said about me!"

"I don't know what you're talking about Charlie," I said.

He yelled, "Outside! Right now. Me and you!"

I asked, "For what?"

Again, he screamed, "Outside! I don't take stuff like that. You are in for a beating."

Everyone just stood there watching. I said, "OK. I don't think this is necessary, but if you want to do it."

When we got to the door, he pushed his finger right into my chest. It was the last move he made. I knocked him out with one swing. I knocked him right out the door. He had his car parked next to the door, and when he fell out the door, his head hit the back tire of the car. I thought he was out, but I wasn't going to take any chances and let him get up. I really worked him over. I really beat him. I guess you'd call it "Ground and Pound."

I'm not glad that I beat up Charlie. I hated to do it. I didn't want to do it, especially in front of all the people who worked at the theater, and in front of several gals who were trying out for the show.

Just a few hours after our fight, people all over town started calling me, saying, "Man, congratulations! We are so glad you did that!" I went into a couple restaurants that week, and they offered to pay for my meal because of it. Anita and her husband eventually left Branson. They moved to Pigeon Forge to start a theater there, and they ended up having a lot of trouble there too.

If any would-be country music stars are reading this, I'm sure they are saying, "Wow, fighting with Anita Bryant's husband in a Branson parking lot seems like such a glamorous life!"

Believe it or not, most entertainers have pretty large egos. Luckily, most of the country music artists I know (and almost all of those who I hang around with) never let their fame go to their head. And as we get older, life has a way of kind of humbling all of us. I found myself humbled (and disappointed) a few years ago. Here's a lesson for any young country singer who's dreaming of being famous...

When I was having most of my hits, I was asked to be on the Board of Directors for the Academy of Country Music. And even though I was very busy at the time, I always made the time to fly out to California to attend their board meetings. I had always been grateful for the Academy. Of course, I won four ACM awards, including the one in 1976 for Most Promising Male Vocalist.

A few years ago, the ACM Awards were being held in Las Vegas. My wife and I were out in Vegas, and I called the ACM office. I told the person who answered, "Hi, this is Moe Bandy. I'm not trying to get free tickets to the show. We'll buy them. But I would like to get some decent seats, if possible."

Get ready to be humbled.

The gal asked me, "What is your name again?"

Again, I said, "Moe Bandy."

She said, "How do you spell that?"

So I spelled my name for her, and then she put me on hold. After a few minutes, she came back on the phone and said, "I'm sorry. We can't do that. We don't know you."

I thought, "You have got to be kidding." There were so many things I wanted to scream into the phone. But I didn't. I only said, "Ya know, I won four of your awards."

I didn't go to those awards that year. But in 2015, for the 50th Annual ACM Awards, they invited a lot of the former award winners to go to AT&T Stadium in Texas. I probably should have told them to stick their invitation. But I didn't. I went ahead and went. I knew that I would only be cheating myself if I didn't go to see all of my old friends.

Some ACM officials might have forgotten who I was, but I found out that many other folks had not. Just a few years ago, before a concert in Texas, I was introduced to the great actor Tommy Lee Jones. Tommy shook my hand, as he said, "Moe Bandy! You are famous!"

I said, "Well, you are pretty famous too."

After we visited, Tommy got a chair and put it right next to the stage. And he sat there and cheered me on all night.

TAMI

I would like to tell you a little bit about the great wife I have. I've been with Tami more than a decade. She is a really good lady. And she's been really good for me. She inspires me. She's been a big inspiration on everything that I do. Tami has just been a Godsend to me.

Tami also lived in Branson, and she had seen me a couple times around town. But each time she saw me, I was headed into a bar! When we first met, she thought that I was a big drinker and carouser. But I had already quit drinking. I still went to the bars to visit with my friends, but I didn't drink.

The first time that I met Tami, I was in a local restaurant/bar, and she came in to meet someone. I saw her when she walked in and I said out loud, "That's the kind of gal I want to marry."

I was really attracted to her. I still am! I walked up to her and we started talking. Tami's daughter had met me before that, and she told her, "He is a really nice guy. You need to go out with him."

Tami has some interesting thoughts about how we first met. And she can tell them better than I can.

♫

"When Moe and I had our first date, I'm sure neither one of us was in any hurry to get married again. Moe had been married thirty-three years. And I had been married for almost twenty-five years! I had two children who were already grown. Moe's children were also grown.

Back in the 90s, I actually took my family to see Moe's show at the Americana Theatre. My kids were ten and twelve years old. After the show, we took a family photo with Moe. It included me, my kids and my then-husband. I'm sure that doesn't happen very often! He also signed T-shirts for my kids, and they still have those! None of us had any idea of what our future held. None of us.

Later, we both lived at Point Royale in Branson, but we were married to other people. When I took my kids to school in the morning, I would see Moe playing golf with Andy Williams. I also walked the neighborhood every day, and Moe did too.

And we would say "Hello" as we passed each other, but we never had any conversation. My kids did talk to him when they saw him walking.

A few years later, my marriage ended. And so did Moe's. I was collecting donations for a Christmas party that I was helping put on for a local women's crisis center, when I went into a local bar/restaurant and saw Mike Nichols. I knew Mike worked with Moe, and I went up to him to ask them for a donation. I was hoping he would donate some tickets to Moe's show.

While I visited with Mike, Moe walked in, came up and started talking to me. He asked me if I would like to do out for dinner sometime. He also asked for my phone number. But I wouldn't give it to him! When I went in there, the last thing that I was doing was looking for a date. I wasn't interested in dating anybody.

I also had another reason for declining his initial invitation: I had seen Moe go into this bar a few times. It was usually about 10:00 at night. And when I had first met him, I thought he must have been a heavy drinker. I didn't want to go out with anyone like that, so I wasn't too interested. I didn't realize that he never drank when he went to the bar!

One night, my daughter asked me to take her to the restaurant to meet one of her friends. I told her I would drop her off, but wouldn't get out of the car. I had been cleaning my house all day. I didn't have any makeup on. I had my dirty t-shirt and old pants on, and I put my coat on over my old clothes.

But when we got to the restaurant, my daughter said that her friend wasn't there yet, and she asked me to go in to wait with her. Little did I know that she had talked to Moe's guy, Mike. And she'd told them that we would be there! Right when I was getting ready to leave, Moe walked in. My daughter kept whispering, "Just be nice. Just be nice." I sat and visited with him the rest of the night. But I never did take my coat off!"

– Tami Bandy, Moe's Wife

♫

Tami finally agreed to meet me for dinner. We started going out, and she found out that I was not the drinker and carouser that she'd thought I was. We got along real well, and always had a good time together. We dated for two and a half years before we decided to get married on June 25, 2008. And our wedding day was a little bit different than most.

Tami liked to go camping in Arkansas, and she always passed a little chapel on her way there. She called the chapel and asked them what we needed to do to get married. The minister told us to get our marriage license at the nearby courthouse and then come on over. She told him she wasn't sure we were going to do it, but he insisted on making us an appointment for 10:00 the next morning! When she told him that we might need to think about it a little more, he said, "If you decide not to come, it's no big deal."

The next day, I had a show in Branson at 2:00, and I knew I had to be back in town by 1:00. But early that morning, we went to get our marriage license, and then headed to the chapel. When we got there, we found out that the pastor was a busy guy. In addition to marrying us, he also lit the candles, and he was also the wedding photographer! The preacher's wife was our one witness. The whole wedding cost us $125. The ceremony was $100, but we paid extra to have the candles lit and for THREE photos!

As soon as we exchanged our vows (and took all those photos), we headed back to Branson. I did my afternoon show, and neither one of us told anyone! We got married on June 25th and we didn't tell anyone until the 4th of July. Tami even went camping with a group of girlfriends just a couple days after our wedding, and she never told any of them! She never said a word.

♫

We had been planning an annual party that I had each 4th of July at my house outside Branson. I always held the party for my family, friends and employees. We played music all day on an outdoor stage, and the party got so big that we started calling it Moe Fest.

I knew that all of my family would be coming up from Texas for Moe Fest, so Tami and I decided to get secretly married and that we would then use the event as our reception. Since no one knew we were celebrating our wedding, nobody had to bring us a gift. We didn't need anything anyway.

In the middle of the party, I got up and said, "I'd like to make an announcement. We just got married. And we would like to welcome all of you to our wedding reception." Everyone was just speechless!

When I first met Tami, I thought she might be too young for me. And she is quite a bit younger than me. But as we talked, she said that she spent a lot of time with her grandkids. And I thought, well, if she's got grandkids, then she might be old enough!

As I was getting ready to wrap up this chapter, Tami came back in and said she had some more things she wanted to say. I hope it's nice…

♫

"Moe and I get along great. We like a lot of the same stuff. We spend a lot of time together. There are times when we are together 24 hours a day for weeks at a time.

I love watching him perform onstage. I love to listen to his songs. And I love watching him interact with his fans. He loves all of his fans. He treats everyone the same. Some artists are different than the persona they have while they're on stage. Moe is not. The person that you see onstage is the same person that he is offstage. It is him. Moe doesn't put on any fake personality on stage. He loves to sing. He loves the music. And he will never retire.

My kids, Travis and Tiph Anie, love Moe. And my grandkids, Kaden, Kylar, Makaya, are very happy that he is their grandpa. They tell everyone that he's their grandpa, and he always tells them that they are his other kids. He always tells them how special they are. We've taken them with us to a lot of his shows. They love riding on the big bus, and they love selling his merchandise at his concerts.

My youngest granddaughter, Makaya, went to school one day, and one of her friends asked her, "Is your grandpa famous?"

She said, "He sure is! My Papa Moe is very famous."

We do our cruise every year and we take all of our family. My kids and grandkids are so proud of Moe. And so am I. He is just a great guy. He's got a very good heart."

— Tami Bandy

♫

I love all of my step children. We are a very close family. Tami keeps me in line. She has helped me a lot with all of my business stuff. She is a great businessperson, and if you ever need to buy a car or bus, you need to let her do the talking. When I was getting ready to buy my latest tour bus, they were asking $100,000 for it. Tami told me to offer $55,000, and I said, "Why don't we just tell them to give it to us?!"

There was no way I was going to make such a low offer, but Tami said, "I will do all the talking." And not only did she make the offer, but she also insisted that they do an extensive, and expensive, complete inspection. And guess what… they took her offer, and I am driving that bus today!

As we were looking for pictures for this book, Tami and I realized that many had been lost forever. On March 21, 2006, I was on tour in Europe, and I got a strange call that an airplane had crashed and destroyed a bunch of my stuff. I had no idea what they were talking about.

But a twin engine plane had crashed right in the middle of Branson! It killed four people. And the plane had crashed into a storage unit that I had. That's where I had been storing a lot of my family photos and country music memorabilia. When the plane crashed, it caused a huge fire that destroyed most of my stuff. Tami went over and dug through the ashes and saved what she could.

Tami and I live just outside of Branson. Even though I don't work there very often, I still love to live there. I love the Ozark Mountains. I love the mountains and the weather. I really love the weather from April through October. I bought a small log cabin that's about five minutes from Branson. But when you get on our property, it feels like you're way out in the country. I started adding onto my cabin, and now I have a pretty big home. We have a nice guest house that our family and friends use when they come to visit.

THE BAND

An entertainer is only as good as the band members who back him up. And I have been blessed with some of the very best. A couple of my band members have been with me for a long time.

Nick Ochoa has played drums for me for almost thirty years. Nick is one of the best drummers and gentlemen I've ever been around. He's just a great guy. When I hired him thirty years ago, he was playing in the house band at Billy Bob's. Nick was a young guy, and he had a big afro. And that made me nervous. But I told him that I would try him out for a week or two, to see how he would do, and he's been with me ever since, for more than three decades! He became my best friend. I would do anything for Nick.

John Clark has been in my band for almost thirty-five years. John plays steel and fiddle. He is one of the best musicians, and still plays better than ever. John and I went through a tough time with our divorces. He is one of my closest friends in the world. John and Nick are both so talented. I know they could have gone off with any other star, bigger stars than me, any time they wanted. So why have they chosen to stay with me? I figured this was a good time to ask them.

♫

"I had been playing for Red Steagall in Fort Worth. And I was playing in a house band when Moe came to town. He had just one or two hit songs, and he didn't travel with his own band, so my brother and I backed him up on a show. A couple weeks later, I got a call from Rich O'Brien. He said that Moe was needing a drummer and he was hoping it would lead to a full-time job. I said, "I'd love to try out for the job."

I met Moe and the other band members at Billy Bob's in Fort Worth. We did the show, and afterwards, Moe asked, "Do you got your bags packed?"

I answered, "I can pack 'em!" and we hit the road for a solid month. We started the month in Bermuda and then went on to California. We played almost every night. At the end of the month, I finally went to Moe and asked, "Do I have the gig?"

He yelled, "Yeah! Didn't I ever tell you?!" And I have been with him ever since.

I watched "Hee Haw" when I was a kid, and I never dreamed that I would get to meet and work with so many of the country stars that I grew up watching. And it was all thanks to Moe. We backed up so many artists who didn't bring their own band. That was so cool to me. But I would choose playing with Moe over anyone else. Moe is a great guy, and a great friend. He lets me play the way I want to play.

Back when I joined the band, we were all a lot younger than we are now. And it was pretty wild out there on the road. But most of that hard partying came to an end when we moved to Branson.

When you're on the road, you have time to do a lot of partying, and most of the band liked to party pretty hard. But when we started playing Branson, we were doing two shows a day, one at 2:00 and one at 8:00, six days a week. And that schedule brought an end to all of the partying. It was a lot more work and a lot less party.

Moe scared the crap out of me one night in Branson. We were all backstage, getting ready for the show. I saw Moe coming up the hallway, and he was grabbing at his throat. I thought he was playing around… but then I could tell that something was seriously wrong with him.

He had a cough lozenge stuck in his throat, and couldn't breathe. I started panicking and began yelling for someone to come help. Scooter Hill came running up and grabbed Moe from behind. He gave him the Heimlich Maneuver and that lozenge came flying out. He really saved Moe's life.

I know that if I ever need anything, all I have to do is call Moe. I know that he will be there for me. It has been an amazing thirty years, being a member of Moe's band. I wouldn't change anything, and I wouldn't trade it for the world. I only wish it could last another thirty years."

— Nick Ochoa

♫

"When I first met Moe in the early 70s, he only had two guys who traveled with him, and then he would get other players at each town. And I backed him up at one of those concerts, but at the end of the night, he went on down the road to the next town and I stayed where I was. It wasn't until ten years later that I joined him full-time on the road.

Moe's type of music is the ideal gig for someone like me. He uses steel guitar and fiddle, and I get to play both of them. When I came into the band, I was thirty-one years old. Moe was just a little older than me.

One concert I will also remember was at Doc Severinsen's club in Oklahoma City. Doc was the famous bandleader on Johnny Carson's Tonight Show, and in

1983, he opened a nightclub in Oklahoma City He brought in big-name acts, and Moe was one of them.

The club had a big curtain that they lifted as the show began. Moe was supposed to walk out onstage as the curtain rose, but someone had set Moe's mic stand too close to the curtain. When the band started playing and they started raising the curtain, that entire mic stand got caught on it. And the more the curtain rose, the higher the mic and stand went. As Moe walked out onstage, he saw it rising up, and he just kept walking at the same speed he had been going; he didn't run over or anything. He just walked up to the stand and caught the entire thing as it went over his head! He grabbed the mic and started singing, and didn't miss a word. Everyone in the crowd thought it was a part of the show. They were like, "Wow, that rising microphone is a cool way to start the concert!"

I have one funny road story. We had two bus drivers. Ray Kreutziger was the main driver, and Richard Hill was our relief driver. Usually, Ray would drive all night, and then Richard would relieve him in the morning. But on this trip, they switched and Richard drove all night.

The next morning, he pulled into a Holiday Inn in the town he thought we would be playing at that evening. Moe was sleeping in his bed in the back, and the rest of the band were still asleep. You have to remember that this was way before GPS directions and cell phones.

I happened to wake up when I felt the bus stop, so I walked into the Holiday Inn with Richard. When we asked for our rooms at the desk, they explained to Richard that he was in Martinsville, Virginia and not Martinsville, WEST Virginia, where we were supposed to be!

As we walked back to the bus, Richard looked at me and said, "We've got a little ways to go," then he paused, and said, "Moe doesn't need to know about this." We had to drive all day, but we made it to the show on time.

Being a country musician, the highlight of my career was the first time I ever got to play on the Grand Ole Opry. I was playing fiddle for Moe at the time. I used a volume pedal; I put my weight on my left foot, and my right foot was on the volume pedal. You had to stay kind of balanced. We kicked off Moe's first song, and I started thinking about where I was and all of the legends who had stood on that same stage. Then I noticed that my fiddle sounded funny. I looked down, and my right foot was going completely crazy on that pedal! I was so nervous.

Another highlight for me came when Moe asked me to go to the White House with him. We played for a very small party there, where they brought in twenty-five or thirty senators and representatives, and we played and sang for them. To be in those surroundings was quite a thrill. It is something I will never forget.

I went through a kind of personal crisis over twenty years ago. It didn't have anything to do with Moe or the band. It was an upheaval in my personal life. I was pretty down, and out of everyone in my life, Moe was the one who stepped up and helped me through it. He really helped me through a very difficult period in my life.

And just a few years ago, Moe helped me again. We had just gotten through an overseas tour of England and Ireland, and we were in Belfast. We were on the plane, getting ready to fly home. As the plane prepared to pull away from the gate, I got very sick. I had some sort of attack and passed out. My blood pressure dropped to nothing.

By the time I'd recovered and told them I was feeling better, the airline wouldn't allow me to fly. They pulled me off the flight, and the plane ended up having three empty seats, because Moe and his wife walked off the plane with me. He missed his flight. We were delayed for a day and a half. I know he could have had someone else stay with me, but he wouldn't leave me there. He rode in the ambulance with me. That shows Moe's real character.

I can't say enough good things about Moe. Working with him is like being in a family. We are a real family. That's the way he treats us. There are some things that I would have done different in my life. But, if given the chance to go back and work more than three decades in Moe Bandy's band, I would do the same thing. I wouldn't change anything. It's been great."

– John Clark

♫

John mentioned Richard Hill. Richard was my road manager. He started out playing guitar for me, and he ended up being with me more than a decade. He went everywhere I went. He was a great guy. He was also my drinkin' buddy. I could do a whole chapter on Richard, but here are just a few stories.

Somewhere in the mid-70s, Richard was with me on a DC-10. My brother Mike and Butch Kirby were in the seats just in front of me and Richard, and we were coming in for a landing at the Indianapolis Airport. We were about fifty feet above the runway when, all of a sudden, the pilot gave the engines every bit of power he had as he pulled the plane straight up.

When we finally smoothed out, the pilot told us that a small, private aircraft was on the runway and crossing right in front of us! My brother Mike turned around to me and said, "Mama almost lost two of us today!"

Richard Hill said, "I know a place where we can get a good deal on new underwear for all of us!"

We were playing the big rodeo at Kemper Arena in Kansas City, Missouri, and Richard had been hittin' the bottle. He was about half snooted up. One of my band members had brought his wife with him, and I told Richard to take the woman to her seat. She was about half drunk too. They were both walking down an alley, and one of the rodeo barrel racers came running through that alley wide open. They were going as fast as they could, and that horse just wiped Richard and her out. It ran right over them. After a minute, the gal got up and asked, "Richard, what did we hit?"

Richard and I got drunk one night when I was staying with the Britt family in Florida. They lived in the richest part of West Palm Beach, next to the ocean, so Richard and I decided to go swimming. We swam way out into the ocean and had a fun time, but the next morning, when everyone found out what we had done, they said, "Oh my God! There are sharks all over the place out there!" We were lucky we didn't get eaten up.

In 1981, I was asked to be in the Macy's Thanksgiving Day parade. And the day before, I had been playing a concert in California, so I had to take the long flight all the way from Los Angeles to New York City. Richard Hill went with me. He was one of the funniest guys I have ever been around in my life. He could do this funny bark and sound just like a Chihuahua. He sounded exactly like a dog.

Richard and I got on the plane to New York, a big 747 that had a first class section upstairs. We sat up there, and the actor/comedian Mel Brooks was sitting next to us. Mel was on one side, and on the other was Mike Wallace, the famous newsman from "60 Minutes." Richard and I started drinking and cutting up, then Richard started barking like a Chihuahua. Mel Brooks was laughing his tail off. He loved it. But Mike Wallace didn't crack a smile. He hardly said anything the entire trip.

I rode on the Justin Boot float in the Macy's Parade. The float would stop at different points, and I would sing my current hit, "Rodeo Romeo", for the TV broadcast. It was so cold that day. But it was a big honor for me.

As I write this, Richard now has Parkinson's Disease. I miss all the great times we had together, but I stay in touch with him. He is still sharp as a tack. His memory is better than mine. When he heard about all the stories I was going to tell on him, he said he had a few comments of his own…

♫

"1971 was a pretty big year for me. I married my wife and I met Moe Bandy in 1971. I went to visit with my grandmother. Grandma couldn't hear very well. And when I got there, she said, "Richard, you had a phone call. It was from somebody who said they wanted you to play guitar for them, or something like that." I asked her who it was, and she said, "It was something like More Brandy."

I finally figured out who "More Brandy" was, and I went to San Antonio to meet with him. And from 1971 to '73, I played lead guitar for Moe. It was just a part-time job. Moe still had his day job. He was overseeing a sheet metal crew at Fort Sam Houston, and he hired me to be part of his crew. So we worked our construction job together in the day, and played music together at night.

A short time later, when he had his first hits and could afford a little band full-time, he called and asked me to go on the road with him. I didn't hesitate.

One of my most memorable moments with Moe came when I got to play lead guitar and sing harmony with him on the Grand Ole Opry. We sang "Hank Williams You Wrote My Life." I had never dreamed that I would ever get to perform on the Opry stage.

We played a show with George Jones in St. Louis, and I found out that George liked to do an impression of Donald Duck. He would talk in the Donald Duck cartoon voice. And I could do that same voice. After the show, we were all back at the hotel, and George and I did a duet, where both of us sang in that Donald Duck voice. I wish someone had had a tape rolling during that. It would have been priceless.

It was an honor to work for Moe from 1971 to 1984. It was really something to see, as his career skyrocketed. It really turned into a whirlwind. I am proud to have been a part of his career and of his life."

– Richard Hill, Former Lead Guitar Player, Road Manager

♫

Richard Hill was with me at the start of my career. And so was Bill Bowers. Bill sang the second part harmony for me, and Richard sang the higher third part. And it was so much fun doing that. Bill traveled with me quite a bit. He was a good musician, and is one of the funniest guys that I've ever met. He was very special to me, and is still a great friend. And after all these years, he can still remember the night we first met.

♫

"I was working with Johnny Bush. Johnny worked with Willie Nelson, and wrote Willie's big hit "Whiskey River." In 1970, I was playing with Johnny at a little club that was just down the street from Moe's house, and Moe came out on the bus and visited with Johnny. Moe was wanting Johnny's advice about breaking into the business, and I met Moe for the first time that night.

A year later, Moe hired Richard Hill to be in his band. I had known Richard. We were from the same area, and one week later, Moe hired me too. I played bass and sang harmony. At the start of all his hits, it was Moe, Richard, and me. And I stayed with Moe for thirteen years.

One of my most memorable shows with Moe came in the very early days. It was just me and him, and then we'd use whatever other band members would be waiting for us at the show. We were booked to play on an Indian reservation in Thatcher, Arizona, and the venue was a combination truck stop-motel-beer joint. The musicians who met us there were a group called Chief Big and the Scalp Hunters.

When I went up to start tuning up with the band, they said, "Tune up? We don't tune up! These people here don't give a shit what you sound like." And to make it even better, they booked us to play there two nights in a row!

It was so cool to be a part of Moe's career as it went from nothing to the big time. I was there when he got his first bus, and I was there when Moe and the whole band would get the new copy of Billboard Magazine each week so that we could see how far up the charts his latest song had gone. We went from playing the truck stop-beer joint on the Indian reservation to playing a 21-day tour in Europe. We performed in England, Scotland and Ireland, and we played in Germany and Berlin.

We were so excited when Moe got his first couple hits. We would celebrate each one. But then the hits started coming so fast that we almost didn't have time to celebrate. They just came, one after another, and we were doing shows almost every night. The last few years I was with him, we played 240 shows a year. And it was a pleasure working with Moe all those years."

– Bill Bowers, Former Band Member

♫

Ray Kreutziger was one of my road managers. And Ray is one of the best guys who ever worked for me. He drove my bus and was my road manager for years, but he was also a true friend. He was so loyal. He took care of me during all of my drinking days. He was just like a brother.

When I moved to Branson, Ray became the manager of my theater, and he still lives in Branson. I also hired his brother, Dennis. Dennis helped drive the bus and sold my merchandise. He was one of my friends from way back, long before I had any hit songs.

Tony Walter was another band member who was with me for a long time. Over the years, Tony would quit and come back, or I would fire him for one reason or another, and then I'd hire him back. But through everything, whether he was working with me or not, we always stayed very good friends. Tony went on to work for Roy Clark for many years, and he now plays with Johnny Lee. When he heard about my book, Tony asked if he could say a few words.

♫

"I was with Moe for almost ten years. He allowed me to see the world. We traveled to Germany, to Europe, to Ireland, and of course throughout the U.S. I got to meet President Bush and his wife Barbara. All because of Moe.

And when Moe moved to Branson, he also helped change my whole life. I got to raise a family, and I was able to actually be there as my kids grew up. Since we were in one spot, in Branson, I got to be home every night and every morning with my family.

Moe and I have always been friends. Even after I left his band, we still stayed friends. When my mother passed away in 1997, Moe was there for me more than anyone. When he was going through his divorce, I was really worried about him. I helped him get over his divorce. And when my wife left me, Moe was there for me. And he knows that I will always be there for him if he ever needs anything."

– Tony Walter, Former Band Member

♫

My band members are like my family. I am very protective of my band. I don't want anyone messing with them. I am in charge of my band. And while there are some road stories that will always stay between me and my band, there are a couple funny stories that I think you will enjoy.

We were playing at the Nugget in Sparks, Nevada, and Phil Coontz played steel guitar for me. We were at our hotel, and Phil ordered a cheeseburger from room service. He sat in his room, eating his cheeseburger, wearing just his underwear. I should also mention that Phil was a big fat guy.

After he had eaten his meal, he opened his door to set the tray and plate out in the hallway, and just as he bent down, his door slammed shut behind him! And here Phil stands, wearing nothing but his underwear! People are walking by, and he is trying to cover himself with his food tray. Then he walked to Ray, our road manager's room. Phil knocked on the door, and Ray looked through the peep hole. He could see Phil standing there naked, but Ray didn't open the door.

He waited a few seconds, and Phil knocked again.

Then Ray yelled, "Phil, I'm not into that stuff!" Phil ended up going to the front desk to get another key to his room!

Phil was a great steel guitar player. But he was tragically killed. He had souped-up a riding lawn mower, he had turned it into a racing lawn mower. And he fell off of it and was killed. He was only fifty-three years old.

One of my band members, who I won't name, fell in love with every woman who ever smiled at him. If a woman kissed him, he thought he had to marry her. And most of his marriages didn't last long. One day, he came to me and announced, "I am getting married this Sunday!" The girl was about half his age. He asked, "Moe, can you come to our wedding?"

I said, "No. But I'll catch the next one."

John Permenter, our fiddle player, was the biggest clutz in the world. He was a great guy, and so mild-mannered. He was a great singer, and a very good fiddle player. But he was so clumsy!

During one show, he was doing a fiddle solo. He walked up to the front of the stage, and then started walking backward, but he tripped over a monitor and fell flat on his back! His fiddle went one way, and his bow flew the other way.

One night, just before the show, John walked onstage trying to balance his fiddle, bow, and a cup of scalding hot coffee. Nick, our drummer, was sitting on a chair and, somehow, clumsy John managed to spill that hot cup of coffee right on Nick's head! Nick had this huge red spot on his head. He looked like Gorbachev!

John was handsome. He was a great player, and an excellent singer. Some people from Europe came to our show, and when they heard John singing, they were just knocked out. They loved him. And they loved him so much that they asked him to go to Europe to do a couple shows. He ended up going there, and he became a big star in Europe!

John now lives in England. A couple years ago, when I played a concert in Scotland, John was my opening act.

Tommy Detamore played steel for a while. One night, the other band members held Tommy over the hotel balcony. They had him upside down, and were holding him by his ankles. That's how they broke him into the band.

Mike Hartgrove played fiddle for me. He was from Knob Noster, Missouri. One year, Mike helped book us into the fair in Knob Noster, and when we drove up, there were only two or three tractors. There was no one there. I said, "Yeah Mike. This is a good one. A real big fair."

He was so embarrassed. But then, the people started coming in. They brought their lawn chairs, set them up, and by show time, there were over a thousand people there.

Eddy Cason ran sound for me for years, and he did a really super job. He did the sound for all my concerts on the road, and when I started my theater in Branson, he designed the sound system and ran it all. He is still a good friend.

Buster Sharp plays bass for me now. He's also a very good singer and good guitar player. Tommy Rials plays piano for me today. He is a Louisiana boy, he's very good. And he worked with Johnny Lee, so he is used to working the road pretty hard.

I'm sure I will forget quite a few, but I want to thank all of these band members and singers who have shared their talent with us over the years: Wayne Brooks, Mark Boyd, Willie_Hall, Steve Sechler, Don Sasanca, Terri Williams, Kris Williams, Ed Synan, Bill Stein, Bobby Boyt, and many others.

MY FANS

I have been blessed to have so many wonderful fans over the years. We have had such loyal fans for so long. Many of the fans who started out cheering us on in the 70s are still with us today, and now they bring their kids to our concerts. And they also bring their grandkids to our shows! I have the greatest fans in the world.

When I think about my biggest and most loyal fans, there is one name that always comes to mind... Betty Urbanek. Betty lives in Sugarland, Texas, and she has been cheering me on for many decades. She was there back when I was playing Schroeder Hall in Texas. She was there when I had to sing behind a chicken wire fence that they put up in front of us. The drunks in the crowd would throw beer bottles at the acts and the chicken wire would keep them from hitting us! The bottles would hit the fence and just explode. Glass and beer went everywhere, but that was better than a bottle hitting us in the head and killing us.

Yes, Betty Urbanek has seen a lot. I thought this would be a good time to finally ask her why she liked me so much.

♫

"I still remember the first time I saw Moe perform. It was forty-one years ago! He was in Simonton, Texas at a little rodeo, and I was totally blown away. I loved his voice. Afterwards, my husband and three kids all went to say hello to him. He was sitting at a little table by himself. He asked us to sit down and visit with him. And that was the start of a friendship that has lasted more than forty years.

I was so thrilled when he started getting popular, and when he started winning awards and having #1 songs, I was so excited. But the best thing was, he never changed. Even when he won all his awards, he was still that guy we'd met at the Simonton Rodeo. He just stayed an ordinary country boy. He was so kind when we first met him, and he is so kind today, forty-one years later.

I got so hooked on Moe's singing. I took my family to see him at least two or three times a month for many, many years, so I have seen hundreds of Moe's shows. Even now, I could see his concerts every day, and I would never get tired of them. I just love his music. So yes, I am a huge fan. But I am also a close friend.

Any time Moe played at Gilley's in Pasadena, Texas, he was less than an hour from our house, so he and the band would come over and spend the day. They'd relax, take a nap and enjoy some of my husband's good barbecue. And Moe loved my banana pudding.

I am now seventy-five years old, just a little older than Moe. I've been married fifty-six years, and my husband Leroy was very understanding about his wife following Moe Bandy all around Texas and beyond. Leroy loved to golf and hunt and fish on the weekends, so he didn't mind that I was on the road at a Moe Bandy concert. And of course, my husband and kids went to many, many Moe shows.

In 1987, my daughter Lisa was diagnosed with cancer. She was only eighteen years old. At the same time, my husband had been laid off from his job. We were really having a tough time paying all of Lisa's medical bills and all of our usual bills, so Gary Morris and Moe decided that they would put on a benefit concert. They had Darrell McCall, Johnny Bush and a whole bunch of other artists come in for free. And they gave all the money to our family. That really sums up the type of person that Moe was, and still is. He is a true, true friend.

I love all of Moe's kids. I was real close to his first wife. And I love Tami, his wife now, so much. She is so sweet. I loved her from the very beginning, and I told Moe, "Whatever you do, don't let her get away!"

My whole family just loves him to death. I have four generations of Moe Bandy fans in my family. There's me, and my daughter, who I raised on Moe. My granddaughter is now thirty years old, and she was raised on Moe. And now, my two-year-old great granddaughter will see me watching one of his videos, and she will say, "Hi Moe!"

When Hurricane Harvey hit Texas this past August, we got 52 inches of rain where we live. And Moe was so worried about us that he called me every day for a week. That's not something that a "star" would do. But it is something that a dear, life-long friend would do.

When people ask me why I love Moe Bandy, I tell them that there is not another out there like him. He is an original. That goes for Moe Bandy the singer, and also for Moe Bandy the man."

– Betty Urbanek, Moe Bandy Fan

♫

I've also found that I have a lot of fans on the Internet. Of course, I have my official Facebook page. Just look for the blue checkmark next to my name. There are also a number of different Moe Bandy Facebook fan sites, and I'm thankful for the fans who have gone to so much trouble to do those. Bob Mauck started the 'Moe Bandy Fans' Facebook page a few years ago. My brother John also helps him with that, and John also assists with a couple other fan sites. I didn't know Bob Mauck personally, so I asked him why he would go to so much trouble for me…

♫

"A few years ago, I came up with the idea of building Facebook fan pages for some of my favorite country music artists. I wanted each one to have their own site, where their biggest fans could go to meet other fans who also loved that artist.

The first star I had a website for was Donna Fargo, and I ended up starting twenty-three different Facebook groups. I have fan pages for twenty-three country artists, and Moe was one I knew I had to have!

Moe is a great artist. I don't think he's ever gotten the recognition that he should have. I think he belongs in the Country Music Hall of Fame. He is one of my favorites and always will be.

Moe is hard core country. He has carried on the tradition of Ernest Tubb and the traditional, classic country artists. Moe has never changed. He stayed true to his roots. He never sold out.

We add more and more people to Moe's fan page every day. Running the fan sites takes some time and effort, but I'm retired now. I'm seventy-six years old. I also have help, with a number of different administrators, people who can post different things to the fan page. And they all do a great job.

And it is worth all the effort, because we love Moe. And the folks who join our fan page are his biggest and most loyal fans."

– Bob Mauck, 'Moe Bandy Fans' Facebook Page

♫

Tammy Gibbs Shockley helps Bob Mauck with the Moe Bandy Fan Facebook page. Tammy hasn't even seen me in concert, and we've never met in person. So I also asked her why she is such a big supporter on the Internet.

♫

"I love Moe's music. I have listened to him since I was a little girl. I'm fifty now. I love his traditional style. His lyrics, his songs all have meaning, and he is a great singer. He is the real deal. His music has picked me up on days when I might be down. And helping promote his music and career on Facebook is my way of thanking him."

– Tammy Gibbs Shockley, Moe Bandy Fan

♫

Pat Shelton also has 'The Great Moe Bandy Fans' Facebook page, and Charlene Rambo oversees 'The Legendary Moe Bandy Fan Group' on Facebook. Those titles make me sound pretty impressive! But I thank those folks and fans for their support.

Terri Becker is a fan who lived in Pasadena, Texas. She went to Gilley's all the time, and she was a big fan of mine. So big, that she asked me to sign her marriage license! I have actually signed several of those for people who had gotten married that day and then come to my show on that same evening!

I've signed thousands of boots and belts. I've autographed fake legs. I signed a wooden leg for a man and then, a few years later, he got a fiberglass leg and he wanted me to sign that. He took his leg off right in front of me and asked me to autograph it!

I've signed artificial arms. And back in the 70s, almost every woman in line wanted you to autograph her chest. It was no big deal. Well, sometimes it was. But hopefully that permanent sharpie marker has faded off by now.

There have been a lot of kids given the first name Bandy. I have met many people who have named their little boy Bandy after me, and I know about a half-dozen people who've named their girls Bandy.

I still have people come up to me and say, "We named our kid after you." It is an honor. I've had many children come up to me in my autograph line and I'll ask them what their name is. When they say "Bandy", I'll joke with 'em and say, "No, that's my name."

During the winter months, you can usually find me on a cruise ship. Besides being a performer on The Country Music Cruise or Larry's Country Diner Cruise, I also host a special cruise just for Moe Bandy fans.

When you're on those cruises, you really become close with your fans. They truly become your friends, and you get to see them so much when you're on the ship. You see them so much that it gets a little funny. The first time they see you, they are so excited. They come running up and have to get a photo and autograph. They are giddy! The next day, they see you and say "Hello", and we might visit a little. But by the end of the cruise, they barely even say "Hey Moe," as they walk right by you! Everyone gets used to each other.

People sometimes ask me where my favorite place to play is. Just about any place in Texas would top the list. Texas fans love us. They have cheered me on since the 60s, and they still come out for all of our shows.

But another favorite place might surprise you... and that would be Canada. We played a place in the northernmost part of Canada. We had to drive a hundred and fifty miles on a gravel road to get there, and when we arrived, we had to cross over a little bridge. And both sides of that bridge were covered with people waiting for us to get there!

When we went to a local restaurant to eat, people pressed up against the front window, just to get a glimpse of us. They had never had the chance to see a country star with a big bus come to their town. We did the concert that night, and people just came from everywhere.

We also did a concert on an Indian reservation in Canada, and we got to know them all real well. I went fishing with them, and we had a ball. The Native Americans have been so great to me over the years. And their casinos have been such a blessing for us. They have booked us for so many shows.

Back in the 70s, there was a big record distributer out west, and they found out that the Indians were big record buyers. And they would usually buy two copies of every record they liked! Usually, Johnny Cash and Waylon Jennings were the two biggest sellers with the Indian community, but for two years, it was me. I sold more records and did more shows in that part of the country than anyone else.

But the Native Americans could be a very hard audience to work for. They didn't respond like everyone else. They would sit there, real serious. I would be onstage thinking, "Boy, I am bombing here." But when I got through, they all came running up to buy my stuff and take pictures and meet me. It has been a really rewarding thing for me to play for the Native Americans. I love them.

I try to be very personable with my fans, and I don't do that just for show. I do it because I love to meet people. I like to hang out with my fans, and take pictures and sign autographs. I end up getting as much or more out of it than my fans do. I get to know so many great people. That's one of my favorite parts of entertaining: I really feel like I'm meeting my friends.

And I still have fun touring. I enjoy being out there on the bus with the band. I love traveling, I love performing and meeting folks, and I enjoy playing music as much as I did when I first started.

FAMILY

One of the reasons I wanted to do this book was for my family. I wanted to be able to pass it on to my grandkids and great grandkids. I wanted them to have a true record of the life that their grandpa lived.

I'd like to talk a little bit about my family right now.

I've already talked a lot about my brother, Mike. Mike's success in rodeo and my success in country music always seemed to overshadow my other brothers and sister. And I always felt guilty about that, because all of my siblings have been very successful in their own right.

My brother Rusty has always been a success. He runs a huge sheet metal company in Austin, Texas. Rusty was also a great cowboy. He roped and rode bulls. Rusty and my other brothers have had to try to live up to me and Mike, and they have had to put up with people walking up to them and saying, "How is Moe and Mike doin'?" They don't even ask them how they are doing! It is something they have always had to put up with. I wanted to give Rusty a chance to say something about that, and I was surprised with his response.

♫

"I have two big brothers who were so successful. And I was so proud of them. I was also very proud to be their brother.

I knew I had some special brothers as far back as my high school years. Both Moe and Mike had quite a reputation for fighting. Mike even beat up the Vice Principal. And on my first day of high school, I was walking down the hallway when a teacher called me over. He said, "Please don't tell me that your last name is Bandy."

I said, "Well, it is."

The teacher asked, "How many more Bandys are there?"

When I answered, "There are two more after me," the teacher shook his head and said, "I am retiring right now!"

If anyone asks me what I think of my brother Moe, and yes, they do ask quite often, this is my answer…

I think that Moe Bandy is the greatest country music singer there ever was. But better than that, he is the best brother anybody could ever have. I am so proud of him. I've got the best brothers in the world."

– Rusty Bandy

♫

In 1966, when my brother Jimmy was eleven years old, he was running across the road to get the mail, and a car hit him. It broke both his legs and it buckled them both inward. I was with him in the hospital, and he got so mad because they had to cut his boots off of him! He didn't want them to ruin his good boots. But he recovered from that, and he also ended up riding bulls. He was a pretty good bull rider.

But Jimmy was also a genius in school. He was very intelligent. He went on to Texas A & M, and got his master's degree. He went to work for Southwest Airlines. He is one of their head computer guys. He's one of the big shots there. Jimmy also plays guitar and sings, just for fun. He got a little band together and performed at a couple of the Southwest Airlines parties. He has done so well for himself. I am very proud of Jimmy.

My brothers and sisters are all great. All of us turned out good. And I am very proud of all of my family. They are very special to me. To show them how special they are, in 2017 I took all of my brothers and sister on a cruise. We went to Jamaica, Cozumel, and the Cayman Islands.

My brother John is the youngest in the family. He runs a plumbing supply company. I am very proud of him too. John once told me that he didn't think he was as good as me, and I said, "Whoa, whoa, whoa! You are as good as I ever was. Just because I beat on a guitar and sing, that don't mean I'm better than anybody." But that's something my brothers have had to deal with. John had these thoughts when I asked him what it has been like to be my brother.

♫

"Moe moved out of the house when I was five years old. Since he was so much older, I didn't get to know him as he was growing up.

But he took me out on tour with him when I was nineteen years old, and he wore me out. He was playing the huge places, but at the same time, if he had a day off, he would go play at a smaller venue. He didn't care where he was performing. As long as he was on a stage somewhere, he was happy.

Lucky Me by Moe Bandy

Moe took all of our family on a cruise last year. It was the first time in fifteen years that all of our brothers and sister have been able to all be together. It was one of the best experiences of my life. To have our family all together again, it was very special.

We had a karaoke night on the cruise, and some of our buddies talked me into getting up and singing. I picked one of Moe's songs, "Till I'm Too Old To Die Young." And I was awful. About halfway through it, Moe came up and finished the song with me.

When I would tell people that I was Moe's brother, they wouldn't believe me. They'd say, "No you're not."

I sell plumbing supplies, and I had one guy ask me, "Your brother is a big star. Well, what happened to you? You sell toilets."

I said, "Toilets are important. Everyone has a toilet in their house. Some have two or three. But not everyone has a Moe Bandy CD."

To most people, Moe is a big star. But to me, he is my brother. I know he will always have my back if I ever have any problem. And I will always have his back and help him in any way I can. It's been an honor and a privilege growing up being his brother."

– John Bandy

♫

I have one sister. Shirley was four and a half years younger than me, but we are very close. Shirley ran the concession stand at our family rodeo. She has a wonderful family. When I recorded the song "Someday Soon", I had all of Shirley's family, her husband and three kids come into the studio. They got to watch me as I recorded "Someday Soon", which turned out to be a big hit. Shirley and her husband had their own company. They are retired now. I always tell her that she is my favorite sister!

♫

"Moe has always been a true older brother. He is very protective of the people he loves, and he was always very protective of me. He was so protective that I didn't think I would ever get married, because Moe would run away all the boys who came around and wanted to date me! But when he got a job up in Temple, Texas, while he was gone, I was able to meet my future husband. And Moe wasn't there to run him off!

When we were kids, Moe took violin lessons, and he used to play "Kaw-Liga" on the fiddle all the time. It didn't surprise me when he became a country music star.

And when he finally made it, we were all very, very proud of him. We'd watch the country award shows on TV, and when he'd win, we'd all jump up and down and scream and clap and cry.

I remember when Moe played in Wheeling, West Virginia at the Jamboree in the Hills. He was on the show with a bunch of other big acts, and he sat my family right on the stage. When I looked out over the audience, it was just a sea of people for as far as you could see. I was looking out at the same thing he was, and I thought, how can he get up there and sing and not be scared to death? To see 85,000 people cheering for my brother, that is something I will never forget.

I have my maiden name on my driver's license. It says "Shirley Bandy Michel", and I have gotten out of at least two tickets because of that. The policeman would look at my license and ask if I was related to Moe. When I said that I was his sister, they'd let me go!

My youngest daughter was born with Down's syndrome. She is now forty-two years old. But she has always been crazy about Moe. She loves being around him, and from the time she was a little girl, we always took her to see his show as much as we could.

Moe is also crazy about her. When Kimberly was little, he did a big benefit for a Down's syndrome organization in San Antonio. He played a concert with Mel Tillis, and they gave all the money to that organization.

We went on a cruise with him last year. Moe was performing for all the passengers and, all of a sudden, I saw that Kimberly had also jumped up onstage. He had called her up to sing with him. She loved every minute of it!

My brother Moe is just a good, good guy. He is a big-hearted guy. And I love him very much."

– Shirley Bandy Michel

♫

All of us, my brothers and sister, get along great. We all genuinely like each other. We are concerned about each other. We have always been close. We never have an argument of any kind. And if there ever is, I am usually the one who jumps in to settle it and try to work everything out.

I have three children. My kids were all great kids. They were great from the time they were born, through all of their growing up years, and now they are all great adults. I was so blessed to have my children. They are the pride of my life, and they always have been. Today, all three of my kids are very successful. I really respect my children. I respect the way that they have grown up and have handled their lives.

As I write this, my oldest daughter, Laura, is fifty-three years old. Laura is a special person. If someone ever needs any kind of help, Laura will be there. She runs people to the doctor. She is always on the go, helping other people. She has the kindest heart in the world. I'm so proud of her. She is a good person.

Laura and her husband Mark have been married 30 years. Mark is a good father and he is a good friend to me. They have three daughters: Brittney, Chelsea, and Shelby. They are in their 20s, and they are all wonderful granddaughters to me. All three of them are very successful. One of them graduated from San Marcos at Texas State. Another graduated from Texas University. She's a social worker. My youngest granddaughter just graduated from nursing school, and she is already working as a nurse. I also have a great-grandson named Gatlin. He's a great little guy.

In the spring of 2017, as I was starting to write this book, my daughter Laura called me and told me that she had breast cancer. It just devastated me. The word "cancer" is so scary. But then she said the doctor had told her that it was very small, and they had caught it early and would be able to take care of it. I was so thankful that she went and got it checked out when she'd first noticed that something was wrong.

As the spring turned to summer, Laura and her family had to make so many important decisions. Early on, they considered their options of whether to have the cancer cut out or to take radiation, but I told her that I would be there for her any time she needed me.

By June, Laura found out that her cancer was much more serious than the doctors had initially thought. It was very aggressive. I had a bunch of shows scheduled, especially over CMA Music Fest week. I was also supposed to play on the Grand Ole Opry, but I cancelled all of my appearances, and instead of going to Nashville, I headed to Texas so that I could be with my daughter.

Laura ended up having a double mastectomy. The cancer was such an aggressive type that they thought that was the best option. Laura made it through the operation very well, and the cancer was not in her lymph nodes. I spent a week with her and held her hand through the whole thing.

Then she went through chemo treatments, and that is never easy...
but I am so thankful that she is going to be OK.

I was also thankful when Laura told me she wanted to say a few
words in this book.

♫

*"My dad and I are very close. He is one of my best friends. I was only six
months old when Dad started his first band, and I kind of grew up at the same time
that my dad's country music career was growing. I remember when he had one of his
first bands. I was only five or six years old. The band would practice in our living
room.*

*As dad's popularity increased, some of my classmates said, "Your dad is
famous!" And many friends at school started asking me, "Can you get me a T-Shirt
or an album of your dad's?" I was in high school when he won most of his big
awards. All of my friends would watch him on TV and cheer him on. They would
ask me to get his autograph for them. And he always signed pictures for anyone who
asked, and I would take them to school.*

*When I was a freshman in high school, I got to travel with him on his first
European tour. I got to go to England, Germany, Sweden, and Holland. We
traveled with Crystal Gayle. She had her mother with her. We also traveled with
Tammy Wynette, and she had brought her daughter, Georgette Jones, with her.
Ronnie Milsap, Conway Twitty and Freddy Fender were also on the tour. And that
was also the event when Joe Stampley came up with the idea for the 'Moe and Joe'
duet. To be traveling with all of these people was something I will never forget. I
couldn't even imagine being in the same room with these huge stars.*

*There was also an incident that happened in Sweden that I will never forget. I
was in a limo with dad, and when we pulled up to the concert hall, I got out of one
side of the car, and dad got out of the other. But as soon as I hopped out, a drunk
guy grabbed my arm and started dragging me down the street. Dad ran around the
car and started after the guy, but the security guards got to him first and got the guy
away from me. It's lucky for him that security got to him before my dad did!*

*If there was any negative to my dad being a "star", it was that he had to be away
from home a lot. It was sad when he had to miss school functions. I know he had a
lot of guilt because he was away from home and away from his kids, but I think it
was harder on him than it was on us kids. Yes, we missed him when he was gone,
but it was just so awesome to be the daughter of somebody who had this amazing and
exciting career.*

*After I had grown up and had my own family, Dad moved to Branson. And
when my kids were little, we would spend a week each summer with him. It was*

always the highlight of our summer. He had his theater then, so we got to see lots of shows. My oldest daughter even performed onstage with him when she was six and seven years old. She would do a show each day with him.

She would be backstage playing with all the little kids, and then she'd hear him call her out to the stage. She'd go out and sing Billy Ray Cyrus' 'Achy Breaky Heart', and then she'd run off and go backstage and play again.

I don't think Dad will ever retire. And I don't think I would ever want him to retire. He is just so spry and energetic. He constantly has to be doing something. I don't think he would be happy if he ever quit performing. Entertaining makes him happy, and I want him to do it for as long as he can. And I think he can go a lot more years. He is in great shape, and can run circles around us kids!

So how would I describe my father? He is the world's greatest dad. He is really special. He is just a good person. He is very humble, and he is also very spiritual. His family means everything to him. He is so good with his kids and his grandkids. I think he is a great man."

– Laura Blandford, Moe's Daughter

♫

My son Ronnie is my best friend. Of course, I am also very close to my daughters, but Ronnie is my buddy. He works with my brother Rusty in a big sheet metal shop in Austin.

Ronnie is my biggest fan. He knows every song I ever did. He can tell you the year I recorded each song; he knows all of my history a lot better than I do. When Ronnie was ten years old, I sang the National Anthem before a Los Angeles Dodgers baseball game. I took him with me, and we both got to meet all the players in the dugout before the game. When he was a little boy, and on through his teenage years, Ronnie always loved to go on tour with me.

On one of those tours, Ronnie brought along one of his friends. And while I was onstage doing my show, Ronnie and his pal were on the bus playing cards. Two girls knocked on the bus door and asked Ronnie if they could use the bathroom, and he let them on. Ronnie pointed them toward the back of the bus, and went back to his card game… and those two women totally robbed us! They went through everyone's pants and stole everything they could get. Ronnie wasn't much of a guard!

Ten years after Ronnie was born, we were surprised to find out that my wife was pregnant again. We didn't expect it. But it was just a treat. We named our new beautiful little girl Lisa, and she was just the love of my life. Lisa was a special gift from God. My other two kids were older, ten and twelve years old, and they just loved their new baby sister.

Lisa is very smart, and is a very good person. She went to college at the University of Texas at San Antonio. Lisa always made great grades, and graduated with honors. She went to work for a big accounting firm, and has been with them for twenty years now. Lisa and her husband Adolph have three great kids. She has a set of twins, Cameron and Gracie, who're heading into their teenage years, and they have an older brother, Bryson, who plays football. Adolph has been a great husband and father.

I did a video for the song "Nobody Gets Off In This Town", and Lisa was in the video with me. Years ago, I wrote a song called "My Wish for You", and I wrote it for Lisa. It will bring a tear to your eye. It's one of my favorite songs that I've ever cut. It will make you think of your children.

I was a sheet metal worker when my first two children were born, and when they were little kids. They had a father who was a construction worker. But by the time they were ten years old or so, their dad had changed jobs and become a country music singer.

The toughest thing about being an entertainer is being away from home so much. I missed out on so much with my family, and there were many, many times when I was just not there for my wife and children. To make a living, I had to travel. And it seemed like I was gone all the time.

♫

While I was enjoying my success, and while I always had fun doing my shows, I always felt guilty about being away from home. I felt worse about it than anyone in my family did. Many years later, when I talked to my kids about it, they all said, "You were great! We all did good. We had a great childhood."

But it is not easy on the family of a traveling entertainer. When I finally *did* come home after being out on the road for a month or so, I'd be so worn out from traveling. And my wife and kids would have the car loaded up, wanting to take a family vacation to Disney World or somewhere. The last thing I wanted to do was hit the road!

One year, we happened to visit Branson, Missouri. I was playing a concert there, and I took my wife and kids. We stayed in a little motel there for several days, we visited Silver Dollar City, and we also went to the Baldknobbers show.

On another vacation, we took my old beat up bus and drove to Hollywood. While we were there, they were filming an episode of 'The Rockford Files'. James Garner was the star of the show, and my son Ronnie went up to him and got his autograph. Little did we know that, later in my life, I would become very close friends with James Garner.

My son also traveled with me a lot during the fair season. All of my kids went with me when they could be out of school. I'd play at the fair at night, and my kids would ride all the carnival rides during the day.

While I love living in Branson, my one regret is that all of my family, kids and grandkids are in Texas. That has been a burden, especially when I want to be with them during important times in their life, good and bad. But I try to make up for it by going down there a lot. I go down every month to two months. And they also come up to Branson during the summer, and we all have a big time.

None of my children ever had any interest in getting into the music business. They are all fans. They all love music. But they think that one performer in our family is enough! All of my kids are very, very special to me. I really respect my children. I respect the way they have grown up and have handled their lives.

MY GREATEST HITS

I've had sixty-six chart records in my career. I've had ten #1 hits, and forty of my songs made it into the top ten on the charts. When I look back at all the songs we have done over the years, and all of the hits that we've had, it is really amazing.

I have no idea how many songs I have recorded, but I *do* know that I've spent a lot of time in the recording studio. I've recorded about sixty albums. And if there are 10-15 songs on each album, that's a lot of songs that I've recorded.

Let me talk about a few of my most important songs…

I Just Started Hatin' Cheatin' Songs Today – 1974 – My producer Ray Baker found the song. It was made up of song titles. Doodle Owens and Whitey Shafer wrote it. It fit me perfectly.

It Was Always So Easy to Find an Unhappy Woman – 1974 – Whitey Shafer wrote it, and it was one of the best country songs I had ever heard. "Some beer drinkin' devil is holdin' my angel, and I know what he'll do if he's my kind." That is a heck of a line. That was such a great song.

Bandy the Rodeo Clown –1975 – I talked about this one quite a bit earlier in the book. It was different for me. It wasn't the hard core country that I had been doin'. It showed that I could do something different, with a different sound. But it just fit me perfect.

Hank Williams, You Wrote My Life – 1975 – Paul Craft wrote that song. He was a bluegrass guy who played the banjo. He wrote it in a bluegrass style, and we changed it to more of a Hank Williams feel. Weldon Myrick kicked it off on the steel guitar, and that became my signature lick. Weldon Myrick was one of the all-time great steel guitar players. And I ended up working with him a lot. He was on most of my records.

The Biggest Airport in the World – 1976 – I always flew out of Dallas/Fort Worth International Airport. One day, I had just landed there and Whitey Shafer told me he had written this song for me.

Here I Am Drunk Again – 1976 – I had sang it around Texas, and we decided to record the song. Once we released it, every bar in the world had it playing on their jukebox.

She Took More Than Her Share – 1976 – It was very well written, and it was another song that Whitey Shafer wrote. Whitey ended up writing more than thirty songs for me!

I'm Sorry For You My Friend – 1977 – I spent a lot of time with Wesley Rose. I wanted to hear all of his stories about Hank Williams. I always loved talking with Wesley, because he really lived through a lot of the early history of country music. During one of our visits, Wesley said, "There is an old Hank Williams song that would be good for you." And it was "I'm Sorry For You My Friend."

Cowboys Ain't Supposed to Cry – 1977 – I was playing a lot of rodeos, and I had a rodeo clown who was part of my act. When I sang the song, he performed for the crowd. He was a great actor. I remember singing the song at the Houston Astrodome, and when I got to the line, "On my way back to Houston…", the whole place just went crazy.

She Just Loved the Cheatin' Out of Me – 1977 – Another Whitey Shafer song. Another cheatin' song. Whitey was spending all the money he made from all the hits he was writing for me. He liked to drive a Cadillac, and he was always partying and drinkin'. He was livin' a wild life. In 1977, a lot of us were.

That's What Makes the Jukebox Play – 1978 – Jimmy Work had this song out in the 50s. I heard it and thought it was a good ol' country song.

Two Lonely People – 1978 – This was a little bit of a different song for me. It had a little rumba beat. We had gotten into a rut, cutting a lot of songs that sounded alike, and we were trying to break that up a little bit.

It's a Cheatin' Situation – 1979 – I covered this one quite a bit earlier in the book, but it was magic when we added Janie Fricke to the song. It really is one of my greatest hits.

Barstool Mountain – 1979 – Johnny Paycheck had recorded the song. They never released it as a single, but I heard it on an album that Johnny did.

Just Good Ol' Boys – Moe and Joe – 1979 – The timing was perfect for this song, and for Moe and Joe. We didn't have any idea there was so many good ol' boys out there. But every one of them bought the record and came to our shows.

Lucky Me by Moe Bandy

I Cheated Me Right Out of You – 1979 – We cut it and I liked it, but I didn't think it should be a single. Ray Baker kept saying that it was a hit song, though. I thought that there were other songs on the album that would be better. But we ended up putting it out, and it kept going and going and going, right up the charts, and it ended up at the very top.

Holding the Bag – Moe and Joe – 1979 – Joe found this song. It was a perfect follow-up to our first duet.

One of a Kind – 1980 – A good ol' country song. It felt really good. It was one of my favorite songs at that time. I was coming to the end of my record contract, and it didn't get much promotion, but it still ended up being a hit.

Yesterday Once More – 1980 – Jim Mundy and Peggy White wrote this. It was a really good song for me. It mentions all the old entertainers who I loved.

Following the Feeling – 1980 – I found this song. Ray Baker was working with Judy Bailey. She was so country. She was a country girl. And she was a very good singer. She made the perfect duet partner.

Rodeo Romeo – 1981 – Dan Mitchell wrote the song, and he also wrote "She's Not Really Cheatin'." I told Dan some stories about my brother Mike, and he wrote "Rodeo Romeo." Later on, he wrote "If You're Gonna Play in Texas, You've Gotta Have a Fiddle in the Band."

Tell Ole I Ain't Here, He Better Get On Home – Moe and Joe –1980 – Wayne Kemp wrote this song. He also recorded it. Wayne wrote some big songs. He wrote "Love Bug" for George Jones. George Strait also had a hit with that song, and Wayne also wrote "The Fireman" for George. He also wrote Johnny Cash's "One Piece at a Time" and "I'll Leave This World Loving You", which was a big hit for Ricky Van Shelton.

Hey Moe, Hey Joe – Moe and Joe – 1981 – I was sitting next to Conway Twitty on a plane, and Conway said, "You need to cut that old Carl Smith song 'Hey Joe'!"

I said, "Conway, all you do is pick hit songs. If you think I should do that one, I'll do it!" Me and Joe did it, and just like Conway had predicted, it went right to the top.

Honky Tonk Queen – Moe and Joe – 1981 – Joe found that song. He was all high on it. It didn't do all that well, because we got a lot of flak for it. We found out that a lot of radio station owners were gay! And they didn't appreciate the song a bit!

Someday Soon – 1982 – Judy Collins had a big hit with this song. Terry Yarborough played in my band, and he always sang a man's version of "Someday Soon." He taught me his version, and I recorded it. Terry played part-time in my band, and his other job was as a train engineer. One day, the train he was in was hit by another train, and he was killed in that accident. After I'd done "Someday Soon", Suzy Bogguss had a hit with the song too.

She's Not Really Cheatin', She's Just Gettin' Even – 1982 – It was a fun song to do. It was a little bit different, with a different beat, and it is still a very popular song with men and women alike.

Only if There's Another You – 1982 – My sheep song! I always dedicate it to all the sheep in the world. Only if there's another ewe! A good country song.

I Still Love You in the Same Ol' Way – 1983 – One of my favorite songs that I've ever cut. Just a nice song.

Let's Get Over Them Together – 1983 – I found this song and carried it with me on the bus for a long time. When I played a concert with Becky Hobbs in her hometown, I was really impressed with her. I told her that I had a song that I thought would be a great duet. We cut it, and it was a big song for us.

Woman Your Love –1984 – It was a kind of different sound for us. Another one of my favorite songs. But it was in a different style.

Where's the Dress – 1984 – Moe and Joe – I detailed this earlier. I didn't know who Boy George was, and I didn't care for the song, but I agreed to do it, since Joe's son wrote it. The same night we recorded the song, Boy George happened to be in town doing a concert. But we didn't go see him.

Till I'm Too Old To Die Young – 1987 – Baillie and the Boys sang backup for me on the song. Hoot Hester played fiddle on the record, and he played that amazing fiddle ride out on the song. You could just feel that soul as he played that fiddle. Hoot passed away a year or so ago. He'd played on so many great songs. But someone once asked him, of all the songs he played on, which one was his favorite? And he said, "Till I'm Too Old To Die Young." And I was very flattered when he said that.

As I mentioned earlier in the book, Michael Johnson is the one who told me about the song. Michael had the big hit "Bluer than Blue." He had found "Till I'm Too Old To Die Young", and he thought that it would be a good song for me. Unfortunately, as I was writing this book, Michael passed away at the age of seventy-two.

But the song was written by Kevin Welch, Scott Dooley and John Hadley. Kevin told me that song is really a prayer. His daughter has sung it in church. I loved the song as soon as I heard it, but no one would cut it because they said it was depressing. But they weren't really listening to the words. When I played the demo on the bus, one of the guys said, "It is a little negative. It's talking about death."

I said, "No, it's really talking about life."

I recorded the song, and there was just an awe in the room. Everybody knew it was a special feeling, and it became one of my biggest hits, but more importantly, it really moved a lot of people.

"Let me watch my children grow…to see what they become." Those are powerful words. I got a lot of letters from people who were very ill or who had family members who had passed away, and they were moved by that song. I also heard many stories of people who were on their death beds and heard that song, and that it had inspired or touched them.

One of my most memorable stories about the song came from a man who had cancer. His cancer was getting very bad, and he'd decided he would rather just kill himself. So he drove his truck to the woods, and he took his gun with him. But when he parked, he turned on the radio, and my song was playing. So he decided to drive back home. He was still contemplating suicide, when he turned on his TV. An episode of 'Country's Family Reunion' was on, and I was singing "Till I'm Too Old to Die Young." Right then, the man said, "The cancer might get me, but I will fight it and I will not kill myself."

The man's brother told me that story, and then he gave me his brother's phone number. I called him and we had a long talk.

But there was at least one very funny incident about the song: we were doing a show, and a drunk guy yelled out, "Hey, do that one song… let me watch my children die! I love that song!"

You Haven't Heard the Last of Me – 1987 – Blake Mevis was my new producer, and he did a great job on my comeback album. Woody Bowles found this song, and it was a good one. It had a really good feel to it.

Americana – 1988 – I talked a lot about "Americana" earlier in the book, but it really opened the door to so many things for me. Jerry

Kennedy found the song. I love Jerry. He is just the greatest guy. I don't think anyone has ever had anything negative to say about him. When Jerry found the song, it was originally about a truck driver, but he thought that it would be better if we just made it about a regular guy driving through town. Larry Alderman, Rich Fagen and Patti Ryan wrote the song.

I've had a lot of hits over the years. But I could have had a few more.

Whitey Shafer wrote a lot of my biggest songs, especially early in my career. But years later, George Strait started recording songs that Whitey had written. And in my shows, I do a medley of songs that I missed.

For years, Whitey was singing "All My Exes Live in Texas" at parties. I just thought it was a funny song that made us all laugh. I had heard him sing it at many parties and guitar pulls that we had, and I never once thought about cutting it! But George Strait heard it, put a swing deal on it, and it became one of his all-time biggest hits.

One day, Whitey came to me with a song that he and his ex-wife Darlene had written. I loved the song, recorded it, and put it on my next album, but we didn't put it out as a single to radio. Ten years later... ten years... I was playing golf with George Strait.

Excitedly, George told me, "Man, I cut a good song the other day!" He said it was called "Does Fort Worth Ever Cross Your Mind", and I said, "George, I recorded that song a decade ago!"

But George released it as a single, and it was another huge hit for him. And believe it or not, I turned down "Amarillo by Morning"! It's no wonder that George Strait says I am one of his favorite artists!

Dan Mitchell was sitting in Ray Baker's office one day, when I walked in and said, "I've been touring in Texas."

Dan asked, "Do you have a fiddle player?"

I looked at him and said, "If you play in Texas, you gotta have a fiddle in the band!"

Dan went home that night, and wrote the song, "If You're Gonna Play in Texas, You've Got to Have a Fiddle in the Band." Then he pitched the song to me, and like a fool, I turned it down. Of course, the group Alabama did it, and it became one of their biggest hits.

"Amarillo By Morning", "If You're Gonna Play in Texas", "Does Fort Worth Ever Cross Your Mind", and "All My Exes Live in

Texas"… what do all of those songs have in common, and why would I pass on them? Of course: they are all about Texas.

At the time, Willie Nelson was real hot. And he was doing a lot of songs about Texas, so I thought that I would stay away from Texas songs. But it cost me a few hits.

In 1990, I released the single, "Nobody Gets Off in This Town", but Garth Brooks had also recorded the song on his debut album. Garth never released his version as a single, but he got so hot at the time that radio people ended up playing his album cut more than they played my single. But it was a good little song.

GUS

I met Gus Arrendale when I was on one of the Country's Family Reunion cruises. We got to talking, and we really hit it off. When he cruises, Gus always has the biggest suite on the ship. He rents almost the entire top of the ship! And he had a big party up in his suite, and we visited a little bit.

Then I started running into Gus at different events. He has built his Springer Mountain Farms into a really great and fast-growing company. Gus lives and breathes his business! And he has been such an inspiration to me, because of the way he promotes his business. I have never seen anyone in my life who is so dedicated to their business as Gus is. He loves to meet people, especially those who love his chicken. It makes his day whenever people come up to him and tell him that they only eat Springer Mountain Farm chicken! And there is no doubt that Springer Mountain Farm chicken is better than other chicken. By far.

We started talking on the phone every two or three days, and Gus and I became very close friends. We have so much in common. We were both raised in small towns, we both like the same kind of music, and we both have the same kind of sense of humor.

On TV, Gus has become known as "the Chicken Man." And he comes across as this very funny, down-to-earth, always smiling country boy. And he is all of those things. But he is also a little bit different in real life. Some people think that Gus is a country bumpkin. He is country, but he is no bumpkin. He is a lot more cultured than most people think. He is much smarter and much more traveled than almost anyone I know.

Speaking of travel, Gus always travels in his own private plane, and he offers that plane to many of the country artists, when our schedule gets too hectic.

Gus had a great airplane. But he decided that he needed a bigger one. So he called me and said, "I'm gonna pick you up in my old plane and I want you to go with me to buy a new one." Then he said, "Be sure to bring your cowboy hat."

When I asked why, he said, "I want to make sure the plane is big enough that you can stand up with your cowboy hat on!"

When we got to the airport, we walked onto this new, just unbelievable plane. I walked down the middle aisle, wearing my hat. And when Gus saw that I had lots of head room, he yelled, "We'll take it!"

The only thing that Gus loves more than chicken is country music. He loves the older singers, and classic country. He also loves Bluegrass music. Gus has done so much for so many of the older artists. People have no idea how many country artists he has helped. He is such a blessing to so many entertainers, myself included.

Gus is a very successful businessman, but he is also so down-to-earth, and he wants to share what he has with his friends. Gus and I have shared many great times over the last few years, and I can't say enough about what a friend he has become. I like to make him laugh. He has the world's greatest laugh. He is one of those guys who, when you mention his name, people will get a smile on their face.

I was blessed from God when I met Gus Arrendale. I really feel that way. I thank Gus for so many things. He is such a great promoter of our music. When I recorded my latest CD, he would tell everyone about it. We were in Las Vegas together, sitting at a blackjack table, and Gus told the dealer, "This is Moe Bandy. He's got a new CD out!"

On TV, Gus is known for wearing his Hawaiian shirts. And he wears those loud shirts almost everywhere he goes! While his clothes might be loud, Gus very quietly, with no fanfare, has helped so many charities. He is a huge supporter of Piedmont College, and I was so flattered when Gus told me that he was setting up a scholarship there in my name. It is one of the biggest things that's ever happened to me. To think that we will be helping students with their education... and it is all thanks to Gus. And he has also given that same honor to Jim Ed Brown and several other artists.

Besides being a great friend, Gus is also a very cool guy. You never know what he is going to surprise you with next. He has flown me and Tami all the way to New York City, just to eat in Central Park and go to a show.

Gus and I also went to Madison Square Garden in New York City. They were having the Professional Bull Riders there. I had been on a cruise, and Gus said he'd pick me up in Galveston when I got back. My brother Mike is a legend in the rodeo business, and Gus asked me if Mike would like to go with us to New York. I said, "I bet he would love it." Mike met us in Galveston, and we all headed to the Big Apple.

When we got to New York, the PBR asked me to sing the National Anthem for them. So I sang the Anthem in Madison Square Garden. As I mentioned before, Gus is much more of a world traveler than anyone would ever think, and when we went with him, we quickly found out that he already knew all of the best places in New York City. He knew all the hot restaurants, and knew just where to go. And when he gets there, everyone knows him! Gus put us up in a beautiful hotel room. It was like an apartment. We all just had a ball, and my brother Mike loved every minute of it.

When I asked Gus if he had anything to add, I knew he would not be at a loss for words.

♫

"Moe is such a good, easygoing fella. We just hit it off. Moe, T.G. Sheppard and I all formed a little club. It's called The Ambassadors Club. The three of us thought that sounded like a pretty fancy name. But we like to travel together and have a good time.

Moe took me to the rodeo. It was one of the best experiences I've ever had in my life. All of the cowboys love him, and when you go to the rodeo with Moe, you get to go behind the scenes. Going to the rodeo with Moe Bandy would be like going to The Grand Ole Opry with Hank Williams, Sr. Everybody loves him.

Moe is one of the nicest, most genuine people I have ever met in my life. He has no ego. He is one of the funniest men I've ever met. He keeps me laughing all the time. He is also great family person. He loves his children and all of his family.

They say most of us can count all of our real friends on one hand. And I consider Moe Bandy one of those true friends. He is one of the most dependable, honest, and sincere men that I know."

– Gus Arrendale, President, Springer Mountain Farms

TODAY

Gus Arrendale has been a great help with my career. And the advent of Sirius XM Radio has also been a huge boost. The Sirius stations that play traditional country music like mine have been a really great thing. Willie's Roadhouse on Sirius plays nothing but traditional country. And one of the best DJs on there, and anywhere on radio, is Dallas Wayne. I asked Dallas if he had any high praise about me. He said this was the best he could do!

♫

"Moe was playing at a club in Canyon, Texas, back in the 80s. And his band was wild. They were on fire, and the audience was just going crazy for them. When Moe and his band came to town, you knew everyone was gonna have some fun.

I met Moe for the first time that night, and we have been friends ever since. I also met his steel guitar player, Tommy Detamore. And Tommy and I are still very close friends.

Not only is Moe a world class singer, he is a great entertainer. He walks out on stage and he owns it. He has that crowd in the palm of his hand from the moment he comes out.

Moe had a kind of laidback charisma that you can't buy. He loves that crowd, and they love him back. And he has also been able to choose great songs to record. He has always found the perfect songs.

I admire Moe's professionalism, and I don't think he's ever going to slow down. I think he will keep doing what he's doin'. As long as the audience is out there having fun, Moe Bandy will be up there entertaining them.

I love how him and Gene Watson pick at each other. I was with them backstage at the Opry, when Gene came out of his dressing room and Moe looked at him and asked, "Gene, are you gonna wear that?"

Gene said, "Yeah, I had planned on it."

And Moe came back with, "I've got a jacket you can borrow. It's so fancy that it will do twenty minutes on its own!"

Moe and I have become a lot closer over the last seven or eight years. He calls me quite often, and always has a good joke. He'll call out of the blue, and he just wants to catch up and make sure everyone is OK.

He is one of the cornerstone artists that we have at Willie's Roadhouse. He is one that we play every day. And he has so many great songs to choose from. But as a person, Moe is a gracious human being. He cares about people. He is real. He is sincere. There is nothing fake about him. I love Moe Bandy."

– Dallas Wayne, On Air Personality for Outlaw Country/
Willie's Roadhouse

♫

There are also a surprising number of classic country radio stations around the country. They still play the songs from the 60s, 70s and 80s, and I am always thankful when they play one of mine. Between them and Sirius XM, they really helped bring our careers back. And the Country's Family Reunion shows and Larry's Country Diner on RFD TV have really had such an amazing impact on all of the older artists, as well. All of us owe Larry Black a tremendous debt that we will probably never be able to repay.

When I'm not listening to Willie's Roadhouse, I am usually reading something. I love to read. I read three newspapers each day, and I *cannot* go to sleep at night without reading a book. I read everything I can. And I read the Bible a lot. I read the Bible every day.

In 1989, I did a song called "Many Mansions." It talks about "in my Father's house are many mansions." I have recorded quite a few gospel songs throughout my career. I've also done a couple gospel albums. Of course, those have been overshadowed by the drinking and cheating songs I've had.

But I am a very, very strong believer. I believe in God, and I believe Jesus Christ is my Savior. My faith is very important to me. I am not a churchgoer. But I am a strong believer.

My life journey (and this book) started in Meridian, Mississippi. And now my life and my book have both kind of come full circle.

I played the Temple Theater in Meridian in April of 2017. I try to get back to Meridian as much as I can, and I play there every two or three years.

But this past year was extra special. They proclaimed it "Moe Bandy Day." They gave me a beautiful plaque, and they also unveiled a big monument down by the railroad station where my grandpa used to work. The monument is a Mississippi Mile Marker. It thrilled me to death when they did that. I also have a star on the Meridian Star of Fame.

During my concert at the Temple Theater, I thought back to when my mother had won a talent show in that very same theater when she was a kid. I was thrilled to be able to do a show there. They are trying to restore that great theater, and all proceeds from my concert went towards the restoration.

As I sang my songs that night, I thought, "I bet my mom is proud of me. I hope she is."

PARTING SONG

This book opened with a foreword by former First Lady Barbara Bush. I cannot tell you how honored I am that Mrs. Bush would do that for us.

When we started working on his book, I had no idea how close Moe had been with the President and Mrs. Bush. And as he told me one story after another about their friendship, I started to wonder if it might be possible that I could get Mrs. Bush to write the foreword. When I mentioned my idea to Moe, he said, "That would be amazing. But it would be asking a lot."

Unfortunately, at the same time that we were writing the book, both President Bush and Barbara were going through very serious, and at times, life-threatening illness.

So, I waited until the book was almost complete. And then, without Moe knowing, I sent the entire President Bush chapter to Mrs. Bush's assistant. When she read it, she emailed me and said, "This will bring back so many wonderful memories for them!" A short time later, I received word that "Mrs. Bush would be glad to write the foreword." I was overjoyed! It was one more very special gift to Moe from the President and First Lady.

I was also honored to get to know so many of Moe's friends and family members. Over the last year, I interviewed many of those by phone and many others in person. The last interview I did was with Gene Watson. And it turned out to be quite memorable!

I wanted to interview Gene in person. I could have called him myself to set it up, but I thought it would be better if Moe called him. Moe agreed saying, "Yeah, Gene is sometimes in a bad mood. And it might go smoother if I introduce you and kind of warn him that you are coming." Gene had a concert two nights later in Kentucky and I told Moe that I would get there a few hours early so Gene and I would have some time to visit.

When I got to the venue, Gene's bus was parked behind the concert hall. As soon as I knocked on the door, I could tell that Gene wasn't ready to talk. He told me to come back in an hour. I remembered Moe's words, "Gene is sometimes in a bad mood." But I came back in an hour. And Gene welcomed me aboard his bus. As we visited, Gene's mood lightened and he gave me a great interview.

A few days later, my phone rang.

"Scot, this is Moe. I think I forgot something."

I answered, "What Moe? Did you leave out something in the book?"

Moe said, "No. I forgot to call Gene to tell him you were coming!"

That explained it! No wonder Gene was not happy when a complete stranger knocked on his bus door and asked to come on and take an hour of his time! Thank you, Gene!

To get to know Moe and his band better, I traveled to Fort Worth, Texas, where he was playing at Lil' Red's Longhorn Saloon. This is where the REAL cowboys and cowgirls go for a good time. I wish everyone had the chance to see Moe in that atmosphere. When he came into the building, it was like Elvis had walked onstage. Those cowboys and cowgirls went crazy. And they loved him more with every classic hit he sang.

As we were wrapping up our book, I took my wife and daughter to meet Moe in Branson. My daughter was celebrating her birthday, and Moe said that he would take us out to lunch.

Just before we arrived, I stopped for gas at a little station near Moe's house. When I got back in the car, I pointed to the little restaurant that was connected to the gas station. It was called 'Dinky's Diner'. I laughed and said, "I bet that's where Moe is going to take us to lunch."

When we got to Moe's, he asked his wife to call the restaurant to see how long they were open. He asked her, "Do you know Dinky's number?" I looked at my wife, and could tell she was starting to laugh.

So we all got in the car and headed to Moe's favorite restaurant, 'Dinky's Diner'. Yes, it was connected to the little gas station. And guess what… it was great! The next time you go to Branson, be sure to drop in and try their grilled cheese sandwich. It's the best you'll ever have!

As you know by now, Moe Bandy has led an amazing life. Most of his hits and awards came before he turned forty. But his most important, and most impressive work, has come over the past three decades.

Moe's song "Till I'm Too Old to Die Young" touched the hearts of thousands and thousands of people. Of course, he recorded that after his record label said that his hit-making days were over.

When Moe was at his lowest point, alone in a hotel room, thinking of taking his own life, he had no idea that his life was just beginning. He had no idea that he would soon become a close friend to The President of the United States. He had no idea that he would open a theater in Branson and would entertain millions of people over the next two decades. And he had no idea that he would help save the lives of so many children with his children's organ transplant organization.

Thank you for letting me help you tell your amazing story, Moe. I'll see you at Dinky's Diner the next time I'm in town.

– Scot England